GRADE 6

240 Vocabulary Words Kids Need to Know

24 Ready-to-Reproduce Packets
That Make
Vocabulary Building
Fun & Effective

by Linda Ward Beech

■SCHOLASTIC
Teaching
Resources

New York • Toronto • London • Auckland • Sydney
Mexico City • New Delhi • Hong Kong • Buenos Aires

Cover design by Gerard Fuchs

Interior design by Melinda Belter

Interior illustrations by Steve Cox, Mike Moran

ISBN: 0-439-28046-X

2 3 4 5 6 7 8 9 10   40   09 08 07 06 05 04 03

GRADE 6 Table of Contents

Using the Book

Where would we be without words? It's hard to imagine. Words are a basic building block of communication, and a strong vocabulary is an essential part of reading, writing, and speaking well. The purpose of this book is to help learners expand the number of words they know and the ways in which they use them. Although 240 vocabulary words are introduced, many more words and meanings are woven into the book's 24 lessons.

Learning new words is not just about encountering them; it's about using them, exploring them, and thinking about them. So the lessons in this book are organized around different aspects and attributes of words—related meanings, how words are formed, where words come from, homophones, homographs, word parts, blends, and much more. The lessons provide an opportunity for students to try out words, reflect on words, and have fun with words.

Materials: As you introduce the lessons, be sure to have the following items available:

dictionaries
thesauruses
writing notebooks or journals
writing tools

TIP You'll find a complete alphabetized list of all the lesson words at the back of the book.

Lesson Organization: Each lesson is three pages long and introduces ten words.

The first lesson page includes:

lesson words

statement of lesson focus

simple sentences explaining the meanings of the words

two exercises

The second page includes:

lesson words

cloze activity

thinking activity with test prep fill-ins

Writing to Learn component

The third page includes:

puzzle, game, or other learning activity using the words

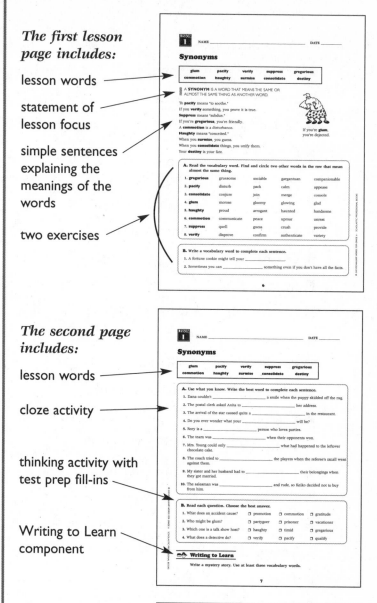

Tips for Using the Lessons:

- Many words have more than one meaning, including some that are not given in the lesson. You may want to point out additional meanings or invite students to discover them independently.

- Many words can be used as more than one part of speech. Again, you can expand students' vocabulary by drawing attention to such usage.

- As you go over the exercises with students, discuss all the choices that are given and why some of them are the wrong answers. In some cases, students may have to look up words in order to determine if a choice is correct or not.

- Have students complete the Writing to Learn activities in a notebook or journal so they have a specific place where they can refer to and review words.

- Consider having students make a set of word cards for each lesson, or make a class set and place it in your writing center.

- Build word family lists with words based on major phonograms such as *glum, clash,* or *chips.*

- Don't hesitate to add your own writing assignments. The more students use a word, the more likely they are to "own" it.

- Be aware of pronunciation differences when teaching homographs. Not all students may pronounce words in the same way and this can lead to confusion.

- Use the words to teach syllabication rules.

- Use the vocabulary words to teach related spelling and grammar rules.

- Encourage students to make semantic maps for some words. For instance, students might organize a map for a noun to show what the word is, what it is like, what it is not like, and include some examples of the word.

- Have students illustrate some words.

- Help students make connections by pointing out lesson words used in other contexts and materials.

- Talk about other forms of a word, for example *pacify, pacifist, pacification, pacifier.* Encourage students to word build in this fashion.

- Have students locate places on a world map when studying word histories and words from other languages.

- Have students categorize words.

- Encourage students to consult more than one reference and to compare information.

> **TIP** Consider having students fill out Word Inventory Sheets before each lesson. The headings for such a sheet might be: Words I Know; Words I Have Seen but Don't Really Know; New Words. Using pencils, students can list the vocabulary words and probable meanings under the headings. As the lesson proceeds, they can make revisions and additions.

Synonyms

glum	pacify	verify	suppress	gregarious
commotion	haughty	surmise	consolidate	destiny

A **SYNONYM** IS A WORD THAT MEANS THE SAME OR ALMOST THE SAME THING AS ANOTHER WORD.

To **pacify** means "to soothe."

If you **verify** something, you prove it is true.

Suppress means "subdue."

If you're **gregarious**, you're friendly.

A **commotion** is a disturbance.

Haughty means "conceited."

When you **surmise**, you guess.

When you **consolidate** things, you unify them.

Your **destiny** is your fate.

If you're **glum**, you're dejected.

A. Read the vocabulary word. Find and circle two other words in the row that mean almost the same thing.

1. **gregarious**	gruesome	sociable	gargantuan	companionable
2. **pacify**	disturb	pack	calm	appease
3. **consolidate**	conjure	join	merge	console
4. **glum**	morose	gloomy	glowing	glad
5. **haughty**	proud	arrogant	haunted	handsome
6. **commotion**	communicate	peace	uproar	unrest
7. **suppress**	quell	guess	crush	provide
8. **verify**	disprove	confirm	authenticate	variety

B. Write a vocabulary word to complete each sentence.

1. A fortune cookie might tell your _____.

2. Sometimes you can _____ something even if you don't have all the facts.

© 240 VOCABULARY WORDS FOR GRADE 6 · SCHOLASTIC PROFESSIONAL BOOKS

Synonyms

glum	pacify	verify	suppress	gregarious
commotion	haughty	surmise	consolidate	destiny

A. Use what you know. Write the best word to complete each sentence.

1. Dana couldn't _____ a smile when the puppy skidded off the rug.

2. The postal clerk asked Anita to _____ her address.

3. The arrival of the star caused quite a _____ in the restaurant.

4. Do you ever wonder what your _____ will be?

5. Rory is a _____ person who loves parties.

6. The team was _____ when their opponents won.

7. Mrs. Young could only _____ what had happened to the leftover chocolate cake.

8. The coach tried to _____ the players when the referee's call went against them.

9. My sister and her husband had to _____ their belongings when they got married.

10. The salesman was _____ and rude, so Keiko decided not to buy from him.

B. Read each question. Choose the best answer.

1. What does an accident cause? ❏ promotion ❏ commotion ❏ gratitude

2. Who might be glum? ❏ partygoer ❏ prisoner ❏ vacationer

3. Which one is a talk show host? ❏ haughty ❏ timid ❏ gregarious

4. What does a detective do? ❏ verify ❏ pacify ❏ qualify

Writing to Learn

Write a mystery story. Use at least three vocabulary words.

© 240 VOCABULARY WORDS FOR GRADE 6   SCHOLASTIC PROFESSIONAL BOOKS

Synonyms

Play Tic-Tac-Synonym. Read each word. Then draw a line through three words in the box that are synonyms for that word. Your line can be vertical, horizontal, or diagonal.

1. glum

trembling	dismal	furious
delirious	sullen	glorious
revealing	unhappy	foolish

2. commotion

sensational	awkward	commune
radiance	corruption	dangerous
tumult	agitation	disturbance

3. suppress

emphasize	revolt	restrain
tempt	stop	suffuse
subdue	supreme	encourage

4. surmise

react	vanish	infer
embrace	surprise	suppose
rebuild	restore	conjecture

5. pacify

quiet	expire	conceal
dramatize	placate	edify
guarantee	paddle	soothe

© 240 VOCABULARY WORDS FOR GRADE 6   SCHOLASTIC PROFESSIONAL BOOKS

Synonyms

disciple	abundant	petition	noxious	surge
impartial	valiant	labyrinth	paramount	haggard

▌ A **SYNONYM** IS A WORD THAT HAS THE SAME OR ALMOST
THE SAME MEANING AS ANOTHER WORD.

A **disciple** is a follower.

Abundant means "ample."

A **petition** is a request.

Something poisonous is **noxious**.

Surge means "rise."

If you are **valiant**, you are brave.

A **labyrinth** is a maze.

Paramount means "most important."

If you are **haggard**, you are exhausted.

Someone who is **impartial** is neutral.

A. Read the words in each row. Write a vocabulary word that means almost the
same thing.

1. plentiful, copious   _____

2. worn, tired   _____

3. courageous, fearless   _____

4. fair, unprejudiced   _____

5. swell, billow   _____

6. entreaty, supplication   _____

7. chief, supreme   _____

8. venomous, malignant   _____

B. Write a vocabulary word for each clue.

1. This word can refer to a student.   _____

2. This word means "a confusing arrangement."   _____

Synonyms

disciple	abundant	petition	noxious	surge
impartial	valiant	labyrinth	paramount	haggard

A. Use what you know. Write the best word to complete each sentence.

1. The fumes from the old machine had a _____ smell.

2. Food was _____ at the fancy buffet.

3. According to this study, there's been a _____ in crime this year.

4. The students took around a _____ for more playground equipment and asked people to sign it.

5. After staying up all night writing a paper, Theo looked really _____ .

6. The judge gave an _____ ruling on the case.

7. It is of _____ importance that you finish all your assignments today.

8. The prince in this tale was _____ and trustworthy.

9. Some farmers create a _____ by cutting paths through their cornstalks in the fall.

10. The _____ met with his teacher every day.

B. Read each question. Choose the best answer.

1. What's a labyrinth? ❑ complicated ❑ simple ❑ straightforward

2. What can surge? ❑ rock ❑ water ❑ star

3. What makes you haggard? ❑ sleep ❑ sleepy ❑ sleeplessness

4. Who is valiant? ❑ coward ❑ bystander ❑ hero

✏️ Writing to Learn

Draw a comic strip. Use at least three vocabulary words in the dialogue.

Synonyms

Write a vocabulary word that is a synonym for each word on the list. Then use the words to help you get through the labyrinth.

1. unbiased _____

2. weary _____

3. toxic _____

4. bountiful _____

5. rise _____

6. dauntless _____

7. principal _____

8. maze _____

9. plea _____

10. adherent _____

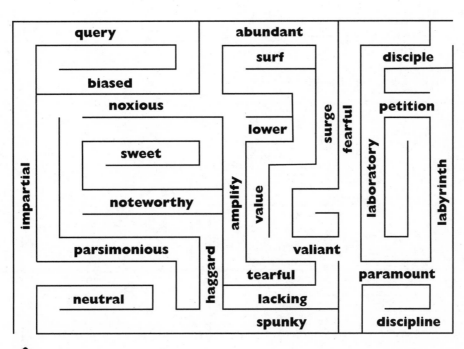

Antonyms

factual	congenial	lenient	entice	transparent
fanciful	**disagreeable**	**severe**	**repel**	**opaque**

AN ANTONYM IS A WORD THAT MEANS THE OPPOSITE OF ANOTHER WORD.

Something that is **factual** is based on facts.

If you are **congenial**, you are agreeable.

Disagreeable means "unpleasant."

Lenient means "merciful."

Severe means "harsh."

Entice means "lure."

If you **repel** someone, you drive that person away.

Something that is **transparent** is easily seen through.

Something that is **opaque** does not allow light or understanding through.

I'm make-believe.

Fanciful means "imaginary."

A. Read each word. Write a word from the box that is an antonym.

stern	impenetrable	reject	tolerant
hostile	real	compatible	tempt

1. **lenient**   _____

2. **transparent** _____

3. **severe**   _____

4. **repel**   _____

5. **disagreeable** _____

6. **fanciful**   _____

7. **entice**   _____

8. **congenial**   _____

B. Read the words in each box. Underline the two words that are antonyms.

1.
> optimist
>
> opaque
>
> obvious

2.
> untrue
>
> falter
>
> factual

Antonyms

factual	congenial	lenient	entice	transparent
fanciful	disagreeable	severe	repel	opaque

A. Use what you know. Write the best word to complete each sentence.

1. Gil felt that the penalty for being late was _____ and unfair.

2. The illustrations for the book were whimsical and _____ .

3. Ilsa tried to _____ the stray cat by leaving out food.

4. The players hoped their coach would be _____ about missing practice.

5. Through the _____ glass, Yori could see the guests at the party.

6. The story our camp counselor told about a monster wasn't at all _____ !

7. Sometimes Kurt's remarks are so _____ , I can't understand him.

8. Everyone on the trip was _____ and got along very well.

9. The realtor worried that the musty odor in the vacant house would _____ potential buyers.

10. When the woman got ahead of her in line, Tanya said something _____

B. Read each question. Choose the best answer.

1. What is a blizzard?   ❐ congenial   ❐ lenient   ❐ severe

2. Which one is disagreeable?   ❐ argument   ❐ conversation   ❐ chat

3. Which one is fanciful?   ❐ hippo   ❐ gryphon   ❐ crocodile

4. Which is most transparent?   ❐ gauze   ❐ wool   ❐ denim

✏ Writing to Learn

Write a factual account of a sports event. Then write a fanciful account of the same event.

Antonyms

Rewrite Nolan's e-mail to his friend, Clay. Use an antonym for each underlined word.

Clay,

Are you lucky that your parents are so <u>severe!</u> They are way <u>disagreeable</u> folks. That <u>factual</u> story about getting caught on a tree branch just made me chuckle. Did they really believe that's why you couldn't get home in time to help with the yard work? It was a very <u>opaque</u> excuse. Maybe next time they'll be able to <u>repel</u> you to help with some cool promises or something.

Nolan

_____

_____

_____

_____

_____

_____

_____

Antonyms

malice	slovenly	mandatory	reverence	posterity
kindness	immaculate	unnecessary	disrespect	ancestors

▍ AN **ANTONYM** IS A WORD THAT MEANS THE
OPPOSITE OF ANOTHER WORD.

Malice is ill will.

When you show **kindness**, you act in a considerate way.

Slovenly means "messy and dirty."

If you are **immaculate**, you are very clean.

Something that is **mandatory** is required.

Something that is **unnecessary** isn't needed.

Reverence means "deep respect."

If someone shows **disrespect**, that person acts rudely.

Posterity refers to generations of the future.

Ancestors are people in
your family from whom you
are descended.

A. Read the word in the first column. Find and circle the word in the row that
is an antonym.

1. **unnecessary**	needless	unfulfilled	needed
2. **slovenly**	slowly	softly	neat
3. **ancestors**	antecedents	descendants	relatives
4. **disrespect**	carelessness	respect	impoliteness
5. **posterity**	forefathers	progeny	possibility

B. Read the word in the first column. Circle the word in the row that is an antonym,
and underline the word that is a synonym.

1. **reverence**	reverend	veneration	discourtesy
2. **kindness**	idleness	consideration	meanness
3. **immaculate**	unsoiled	unkempt	disruptive
4. **malice**	spite	hunger	love
5. **mandatory**	unneeded	obligatory	tolerant

Antonyms

malice	slovenly	mandatory	reverence	posterity
kindness	immaculate	unnecessary	disrespect	ancestors

A. Use what you know. Write the best word to complete each sentence.

1. The doctor showed great gentleness and _____ while treating the confused man.

2. At training camp, a swim before breakfast was a _____ exercise.

3. The rusty, abandoned cars in the yard gave the place a _____ look.

4. Mom said that a new shirt was _____ because Dennis had plenty of shirts.

5. The students made family trees and listed their _____ on them.

6. Talking during a play is a sign of _____ to the actors and other members of the audience.

7. In her crisp uniform, the nurse looked neat and _____ .

8. "I hope my work will be read by _____ ," the author told the interviewer.

9. The followers spoke with great _____ for their beloved leader.

10. The demonstrators were angry and showed _____ toward their opposition.

B. Read each question. Choose the best answer.

1. Who inherits?   ❏ posterity   ❏ ancestors   ❏ contemporaries

2. Who shows malice?   ❏ friend   ❏ acquaintance   ❏ enemy

3. What's unnecessary?   ❏ eating   ❏ sleeping   ❏ teasing

4. What does a boor show?   ❏ reverence   ❏ disrespect   ❏ manners

✏ Writing to Learn

Write a letter of advice to be read by posterity. Use at least three vocabulary words.

Antonyms

Write the vocabulary word for each clue. Then write the circled letters on the numbered lines at the bottom of the page to answer the riddle.

WHAT DO CATS EAT WHEN THEY'RE IN A HURRY?

1. superfluous

2. great-great-great grandparent

3. doing good

4. a desire to harm someone

5. necessary

6. unsullied

7. rudeness

8. adoration

9. sloppy

10. offspring

___   ___   ___   ___   ___   ___   ___   ___   ___   ___   ___

 4   3   5   1   10   8   6   7   2   9

Compound Words

high-rise	open-ended	drive-in	troubleshoot	life span
solar energy	know-how	low-key	getaway	health club

> A **COMPOUND WORD** IS MADE UP OF TWO OR MORE WORDS PUT TOGETHER. A COMPOUND WORD CAN BE WRITTEN AS ONE WORD OR AS TWO SEPARATE WORDS. SOME COMPOUND WORDS ARE HYPHENATED.

A **high-rise** is a building with many stories.

When something is **open-ended**, it is not final.

A **drive-in** is a place where people get served while in their cars.

When you **troubleshoot**, you eliminate problems.

Energy from the sun is **solar energy**.

Know-how means "expertise."

If something is **low-key**, it is played down.

A **getaway** is an exit.

A **health club** is a place with exercise equipment.

Your **life span** is the length of your life.

A. Draw a line to match each vocabulary word with its meaning.

1. **high-rise**   a. lifetime

2. **life span**   b. understated

3. **open-ended**   c. rectify

4. **getaway**   d. skyscraper

5. **drive-in**   e. inconclusive

6. **troubleshoot**   f. escape

7. **know-how**   g. restaurant

8. **low-key**   h. capability

B. Write a vocabulary word for each picture.

1.

_____

2.

_____

Compound Words

high-rise	open-ended	drive-in	troubleshoot	life span
solar energy	know-how	low-key	getaway	health club

A. Use what you know. Write the best word to complete each sentence.

1. An Asian elephant has a _____ of up to 80 years.

2. The Pappos family moved to the twentieth floor of a new _____ .

3. Dad's job at the fair was to _____ and solve any issues.

4. Several questions on the test were _____ and had no one answer.

5. This building is heated by _____ .

6. Conchita takes a stretching class at the _____ twice a week.

7. When it comes to repairing cars, Cyrus has a lot of _____ .

8. The van in the photo is the one the robbers used in their _____ .

9. The singer was _____ and not at all flashy.

10. On our trip, we bought lunch at a _____ so we didn't lose time.

B. Read each question. Choose the best answer.

1. Where do you run? ☐ high rise ☐ health care ☐ health club

2. What's good for a getaway? ☐ cart ☐ car ☐ carton

3. Who has know-how? ☐ novice ☐ student ☐ expert

4. Where can you get cash? ☐ drive-in ☐ run-in ☐ shut-in

✏ Writing to Learn

Pretend you are a real estate broker. Write a brochure for your community. Include at least three vocabulary words.

Compound Words

Read each list of words. Write a vocabulary word to go with each group.

1.   nutrition

                spa

           bench-pressing

_____

2.   existence

            duration

            survival

_____

3.   flight

           departure

           elude

_____

4.   restrained

           underemphasized

           inhibited

_____

5.   power

           electricity

           rays

_____

6.   correct

           eliminate

           resolve

_____

7.   many-storied

           tall

           elevators

_____

8.   fast food

           automobile

           convenience

_____

9.   uncommitted

           limitless

           undecided

_____

10.   skill

           proficiency

           ability

_____

Homophones

sari	waver	hostel	hue	insight
sorry	waiver	hostile	hew	incite

▌ A **HOMOPHONE** IS A WORD THAT SOUNDS LIKE ANOTHER WORD
BUT HAS A DIFFERENT MEANING, SPELLING, AND ORIGIN.

A **sari** is a garment worn by Hindu women.

If you are **sorry**, you are apologetic.

When you **waver**, you hesitate.

A **waiver** is a document that gives up a claim.

A **hostel** is an inexpensive lodging.

Hue is a gradation of color.

If you **hew** something, you chop or cut it out.

Insight is the ability to understand something.

To **incite** is to stir up.

Hostile means "unfriendly."

A. Read the words in each row. Write the vocabulary word that means almost the same thing.

1. tint, shade   _____

2. vacillate, fluctuate

   _____

3. rancorous, antagonistic

   _____

4. regretful, remorseful

   _____

5. carve, cleave   _____

6. provoke, arouse

   _____

7. intuition, perception

   _____

B. Complete each riddle with a vocabulary word. Use the pictures to help you.

1.    I sound like *hostile*, but I am a

   _____ .

2.    I sound like *sorry*, but I am a

   _____ .

3.   I sound like *waver*, but I am a

   _____ .

NAME _____   DATE _____

Homophones

sari	waver	hostel	hue	insight
sorry	waiver	hostile	hew	incite

A. Use what you know. Write the best word to complete each sentence.

1. The sky's _____ deepened as the sun set.

2. The hikers stopped for the night at a youth _____ .

3. Did the leaders try to _____ the workers to trouble?

4. Fatima wrapped a beautiful yellow _____ around her.

5. You could see the deer _____ as we interrupted their meal of our yew bushes.

6. The carver began to _____ a figure from the wood.

7. With sudden _____ , Kaneko knew what she had to do.

8. Jill was _____ she had been so rude to the caller.

9. Mr. Fine agreed to a _____ relinquishing his right to the property.

10. The crowd seemed angry and _____ to the visiting dignitaries.

B. Read each question. Choose the best answer.

1. What might a dieter do?   ❒ wave   ❒ waver   ❒ waiver

2. Who says sorry?   ❒ offender   ❒ offended   ❒ offensive

3. What hue is the ocean?   ❒ purple   ❒ orange   ❒ blue

4. How do enemies feel?   ❒ hostel   ❒ hostile   ❒ hospitable

 Writing to Learn

Write an apology that one neighbor might make to another. Use at least three vocabulary words.

© 240 VOCABULARY WORDS FOR GRADE 6   SCHOLASTIC PROFESSIONAL BOOKS

NAME _____   DATE _____

Homophones

These book titles have errors in them. Rewrite each title so it is correct.

1.

Mystery
at the Hostel
Hostile

_____
_____
_____

2.

If You Sign
a Waver,
You Might
Be Sari

_____
_____
_____

3.

Incite
into Hews
for Your
Home

_____
_____
_____

4.

Looking
Good
in a
Sorry

_____
_____
_____

5.

Don't Waiver!
How to Hue
Out Your Share
of Happiness

_____
_____
_____

6.

When to
Insight a
Rebellion

_____
_____
_____

NAME _____ DATE _____

Homographs

wound	buffet	incense	pawn	intimate
wound	buffet	incense	pawn	intimate

A **HOMOGRAPH** IS A WORD THAT IS SPELLED THE SAME AS ANOTHER WORD BUT HAS A DIFFERENT MEANING AND SOMETIMES A DIFFERENT PRONUNCIATION.

Wound is the past tense of *wind*, meaning "to wrap around."

A **buffet** is a counter from which meals are served.

To **buffet** is to strike forcefully.

Incense is a substance that burns with a strong odor.

If you **incense** someone, you anger that person.

A **pawn** is the lowest piece in a chess game.

If you **pawn** something, you give it as a deposit for a loan.

Intimate means "a close association."

If you **intimate** something, you give a hint.

A **wound** is an injury.

A. Read each sentence. Then circle the correct pronunciation of the word.

1. Did the boss **intimate** that Troy was getting a raise?   **a.** in' tə māt   **b.** in' tə mət

2. Anita often burned **incense** on the porch.   **a.** in' sen(t)s   **b.** in sen(t)s'

3. The restaurant had a huge **buffet** on Saturday nights.   **a.** bə fā'   **b.** bə fət'

4. Be careful not to **incense** the bear.   **a.** in' sen(t)s   **b.** in sen(t)s'

5. That storm will **buffet** the ships at sea.   **a.** bə fā'   **b.** bə fət'

6. The friends had known each other for years and were on **intimate** terms.   **a.** in' tə māt   **b.** in' tə mət

---

B. Write a vocabulary word for each underlined word or words.

1. Bruce moved a <u>chess piece</u> and then waited.   _____

2. The doctor tended to the patient's <u>injury</u>.   _____

3. The dancers <u>spun</u> around the maypole.   _____

4. Neil decided to <u>stake</u> his watch for a loan.   _____

NAME _____ DATE _____

Homographs

wound	buffet	incense	pawn	intimate
wound	buffet	incense	pawn	intimate

A. Use what you know. Write the best word to complete each sentence.

1. Expertly, the mother _____ a band around her daughter's hair.

2. We could smell the _____ as we entered the church.

3. Ruby captured the _____ her opponent had moved.

4. For dinner, an appetizing _____ was set up along one side of the room.

5. Although they lived on the same floor, the two families were not _____ .

6. After stumbling over a root, the climber had a nasty _____ on his leg.

7. Strong winds sometimes _____ the chair lifts at this mountain.

8. It will _____ Dad if we leave the dirty dishes in the sink.

9. The speaker's words _____ his feelings about the situation.

10. When you _____ jewelry, you don't get much money for it.

B. Read each question. Choose the best answer.

1. Can a **buffet** **buffet**?   ❑ yes   ❑ no

2. Can an **intimate** **intimate**?   ❑ yes   ❑ no

3. Can you **pawn** a **pawn**?   ❑ yes   ❑ no

4. Can **incense** **incense** you?   ❑ yes   ❑ no

Writing to Learn

Explain why homographs can be confusing. Give some tips for understanding them. Use at least three homographs as examples.

Homographs

Show that you are a homograph hound. Read each sentence. Circle the number beside the correct meaning for each boldfaced word. If the numbers add up to 20, you're a winner and a homograph hound.

A. The photograph shows an **intimate** family gathering.

      1. suggested   **2.** close   **3.** interior

B. Let's take the flag down so the wind doesn't **buffet** it too much.

      1. food service   **2.** batter   **3.** bother

C. The vet treated the dog's **wound**.

      1. damaged flesh   **2.** twirled around   **3.** illness

D. Judy bought several sticks of **incense**.

      1. intense   **2.** infuriate   **3.** aromatic substance

E. Did the host **intimate** that the party was over?

      1. affectionate   **2.** imply   **3.** instigate

F. The path **wound** through a field and up a hill.

      1. injury   **2.** bumped   **3.** twisted

G. As the player set up the board, one of the **pawns** fell.

      1. chess pieces   **2.** shrimp   **3.** exchange for a loan

H. The shoppers were **incensed** when the store ran out of the sale item.

      1. perfumed   **2.** encouraged   **3.** enraged

I. More people come in to **pawn** things at the end of the month.

      1. make security deposit   **2.** play a board game   **3.** display

J. We heaped our plates with selections from the **buffet**.

      1. hit hard   **2.** food table   **3.** basket

Eponyms: People

derrick	zinnia	cardigan	maverick	boycott
mesmerize	saturnine	laconic	sequoia	bacitracin

▌ AN **EPONYM** IS A WORD THAT COMES FROM
THE NAME OF A PERSON OR PLACE.

Mesmerize means "to hypnotize."

A **derrick** is a large crane.

A **zinnia** is a colorful flower.

A **cardigan** is a sweater that buttons in front.

A **maverick** is someone who doesn't go along with a group's thinking.

If you **boycott** something, you stop using it.

Saturnine means "gloomy." / Someone who is **laconic** uses few words.

A **sequoia** is a giant redwood tree. / **Bacitracin** is an antibiotic ointment.

A. Write a vocabulary word for each sentence.

1. Saturn was a god in Roman myths.   _____

2. Sequoya, a Cherokee, created a system of writing for his people   _____
in 1821.

3. The Laconians of ancient Greece were known for their brief speech.   _____

4. An Austrian doctor, Franz Mesmer, used hypnotism to treat patients.   _____

5. J.T. Brudenell, the Earl of Cardigan, wore a sweater that was open   _____
in the front.

6. Samuel A. Maverick was a Texas cattleman who didn't brand his   _____
calves when other ranchers did.

B. Draw a line to match each word with its name story.

1. bacitracin   **a.** In 1600, a gallows in England was named for Derick,
a famous hangman.

2. boycott   **b.** Botanist Johann Zinn discovered a flower.

3. derrick   **c.** When Captain Charles Boycott raised rents on an estate
in Ireland, the tenants turned against him.

4. zinnia   **d.** An antibody in the blood of Margaret Tracy led to an ointment
that fights infections.

NAME _____   DATE _____

Eponyms: People

derrick	zinnia	cardigan	maverick	boycott
mesmerize	saturnine	laconic	sequoia	bacitracin

A. Use what you know. Write the best word to complete each sentence.

1. People threatened to _____ the store because of its policies.

2. Gwen took along a _____ in case the day got cooler.

3. The main character in the movie seemed glum and _____ to the viewers.

4. The oil field was crowded with _____ .

5. The nurse applied _____ to Ziggy's cut.

6. By late summer, Mom's garden is bright with _____ .

7. The children were _____ by the musician and sat there listening for hours.

8. A national park in California is noted for its stands of _____ trees.

9. She is very original and something of a _____ in her field.

10. Devon's response to the question was short and _____ .

B. Read each question. Choose the best answer.

1. Who boycotts?   ❏ supporters   ❏ protesters   ❏ bystanders

2. Which one buttons?   ❏ turtleneck   ❏ pullover   ❏ cardigan

3. Which one's an annual?   ❏ sequoia   ❏ zinnia   ❏ pecan tree

4. What does a maverick do? ❏ dissent   ❏ consent   ❏ relent

✎ Writing to Learn

Find out more about the history of one of the vocabulary words and the person for whom it is named. Write a paragraph to report on your research.

Eponyms: People

Read the clues. Then find and circle each word in the puzzle. Write the word next to the clue.

1. the tallest tree _____

2. a warm and wooly wrap _____

3. avoid _____

4. not wordy _____

5. named for a patient _____

6. put in a trance _____

7. nice in a bouquet _____

8. dismal and morose _____

9. an unconventional person _____

10. named for a hangman _____

```
D  F  W  N  L  U  B  J  L  V  C  M
M  X  T  S  A  T  U  R  N  I  N  E
O  P  C  G  C  K  R  Y  B  S  H  S
B  O  Y  C  O  T  T  A  F  G  I  M
A  T  J  O  N  D  E  X  M  C  U  E
C  Z  D  Z  I  N  N  I  A  L  E  R
I  A  M  H  C  Q  W  J  V  P  T  I
T  V  D  U  D  R  Z  T  E  K  N  Z
R  S  E  C  T  N  B  T  R  L  C  E
A  J  R  Y  Z  S  X  H  I  J  W  F
C  A  R  D  I  G  A  N  C  I  B  V
I  G  I  C  F  K  O  R  K  E  V  O
N  G  C  M  Y  I  K  B  U  P  L  X
R  Q  K  W  A  S  E  Q  U  O  I  A
```

Eponyms: Places

afghan	badminton	cashmere	currants	spaniel
denim	atoll	turquoise	canary	mayonnaise

▎AN **EPONYM** IS A WORD THAT COMES FROM
THE NAME OF A PERSON OR PLACE.

An **afghan** is a blanket knitted or crocheted in a colorful pattern.

Badminton is a game played over a net.

Cashmere is a soft wool that comes from a goat.

Currants are small berries. / A **spaniel** is a kind of dog.

Denim is a heavy cloth used in making overalls.

An **atoll** is a coral island. / **Turquoise** is a blue-green gemstone.

Mayonnaise is a dressing made from oil and egg yolk.

A **canary** is a yellow songbird.

A. Write the word from the box that goes with each sentence.

afghan	currants	atoll	canary	denim	turquoise

1. This yellow finch is from the Canary Islands off western Africa.   _____

2. This fruit was named for the city of Corinth in ancient Greece.   _____

3. The word for this stone comes from the country of Turkey.   _____

4. This covering gets its name from the country of Afghanistan.   _____

5. This blue cloth came from a French town called Nîmes.   _____

6. The native word for the Maldive Islands is *atolu*, meaning "reef."   _____

B. Draw a line to match each word with its name story.

1. badminton

2. cashmere

3. mayonnaise

4. spaniel

a. A canine prized for its dancing came from España (Spain).

b. A French duke celebrated his capture of the city of Mahón in 1756.

c. A racquet game was first played at a British estate called Badminton.

d. Goats native to Kashmir lent their name to this wool.

Eponyms: Places

afghan	badminton	cashmere	currants	spaniel
denim	atoll	turquoise	canary	mayonnaise

A. Use what you know. Write the best word to complete each sentence.

1. Before going out, Mr. Durand wrapped a warm _____ scarf around his neck.

2. Fiona got a _____ ring for her birthday.

3. A cage hung by the window, and in it was a little _____ .

4. The small boat moved slowly along the reef of the _____ .

5. Our dog Scruffy is a brown and white _____ .

6. We made jelly from the _____ Dad picked.

7. The uniforms of most mechanics are made from sturdy _____ .

8. The cook added _____ to the chicken to make a salad.

9. Some of the guests played a game of _____ before the barbecue.

10. Jenna has a bright _____ on her bed that her aunt made.

B. Read each question. Choose the best answer.

1. Which one's in the ocean? ❏ currant ❏ turquoise ❏ atoll

2. What are jeans made from? ❏ denim ❏ cashmere ❏ afghan

3. Which one flies? ❏ canasta ❏ canary ❏ cannery

4. Where do you use mayonnaise? ❏ sandwich ❏ cereal ❏ cake

✏ Writing to Learn

Pretend you are writing the copy for a catalog. Choose at least three items that are vocabulary words, and write catalog copy for them.

Eponyms: Places

Read the clues. Then complete the puzzle.

1. has droopy ears and a silky coat

2. an island made of coral

3. a patterned coverlet

4. a feathered pet

5. a white dressing

6. berries used in buns

7. game named for an English estate

8. used for making sweaters

9. strong fabric

10. stone often used in Navajo jewelry

```
1. ___  P  ___ ___ ___ ___ ___
   2. ___ ___ ___ ___  L
      3. ___ ___ ___ ___  A  ___
         4.  C  ___ ___ ___ ___ ___
5. ___ ___ ___ ___ ___ ___ ___ ___  E  ___
      6. ___ ___ ___ ___ ___  N  ___ ___
         7. ___  A  ___ ___ ___ ___ ___ ___
      8. ___ ___ ___ ___  M  ___ ___
         9. ___  E  ___ ___
   10. ___ ___ ___ ___ ___ ___ ___  S  ___
```

© 240 VOCABULARY WORDS FOR GRADE 6   SCHOLASTIC PROFESSIONAL BOOKS

NAME _____   DATE _____

Words From Other Languages

scow	loiter	algebra	poodle	orangutan
frolic	iceberg	safari	snorkel	sarong

MANY WORDS IN ENGLISH COME FROM OTHER LANGUAGES.

Words From Dutch   A **scow** is a flat-bottomed boat.

If you **frolic**, you play in a frisky way.

When you **loiter**, you linger.

An **iceberg** is a large mass of floating ice that has broken off from a glacier.

(From Dutch)

Words From Arabic   **Algebra** is a branch of mathematics in which letters are used to represent sets of numbers.

A **safari** is a hunting or exploring trip.

Words From German   A **poodle** is a type of dog.

A **snorkel** is a German word for a breathing tube for swimmers.

Words From Malay   An **orangutan** is an ape that lives in trees.

A **sarong** is a cloth that is wrapped and worn as a skirt.

A. Write *Dutch, Arabic, German,* or *Malay* to tell where the word for each picture is from.

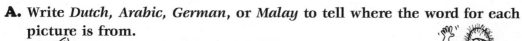

1.  _____

2. _____

3.  _____

4.  _____

5.  _____

6. 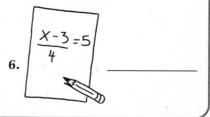 _____

B. Read the words. Write a vocabulary word that means almost the same thing.

1. romp, cavort   _____   2. dally, dawdle   _____

3. barge, flatboat   _____   4. expedition, exploration   _____

Words From Other Languages

scow	loiter	algebra	poodle	orangutan
frolic	iceberg	safari	snorkel	sarong

A. Use what you know. Write the best word to complete each sentence.

1. The guide led tourists on a _____ to see wild animals in Africa.

2. The vet clipped the thick curly hair on Barry's pet _____ .

3. Come straight home from school and don't _____ anywhere.

4. In 1912, the *Titanic* hit an _____ in the North Atlantic Ocean.

5. Ruth did her _____ homework and then checked her equations.

6. The _____ is a common garment on many Pacific Islands.

7. Through the pet show window, we could see the puppies _____ and play.

8. A _____ carrying a load of coal moved slowly up the river.

9. The swimming instructor demonstrated how to use the mask and _____ .

10. The large hairy red ape called an _____ comes from the rain forests of Sumatra and Borneo.

B. Read each question. Choose the best answer.

1. Which one do you wear?   ❐ safari   ❐ savanna   ❐ sarong

2. Which one do you avoid?   ❐ iceberg   ❐ icing   ❐ ibis

3. Which one might you buy?   ❐ snorkel   ❐ algebra   ❐ orangutan

4. Which one might frolic?   ❐ puddle   ❐ paddle   ❐ poodle

Writing to Learn

Write the table of contents for a travel magazine. Use at least four vocabulary words.

NAME _____   DATE _____

Words From Other Languages

An analogy is a comparison based on how things are related to one another. Complete each of these analogies with a vocabulary word.

1. A tabby is to a calico as a spaniel is to a _____ .

2. Grammar is to punctuation as geometry is to _____ .

3. A van is to a jeep as a freighter is to a _____ .

4. Gregarious is to sociable as idle is to _____ .

5. A blizzard is to a hurricane as a reef is to an _____ .

6. A hike is to a trek as an expedition is to a _____ .

7. A shawl is to a poncho as a skirt is to a _____ .

8. Lenient is to easygoing as revel is to _____ .

9. A helmet is to a cyclist as a _____ is to a diver.

10. A moose is to a deer as an _____ is to an ape.

NAME _____ DATE _____

Words From Literature

jabberwocky	lilliputian	quixotic	narcissus	robot
puckish	Herculean	utopian	scrooge	malapropism

NEW WORDS SOMETIMES COME FROM CHARACTERS, PLACES, AND EVENTS IN **LITERATURE**.

A **robot** is a mechanical device that performs human tasks.

Writing or speech that makes no sense is **jabberwocky**.

Something very tiny is **lilliputian**.

Someone who is romantic and impractical is **quixotic**.

A **narcissus** is a flower that grows from a bulb. / **Puckish** means "mischievous."

Herculean means "really difficult." / A **utopian** idea is one that is visionary but imaginary.

A miserly person is a **scrooge**. / A **malapropism** is a funny misuse of words.

A. Write a vocabulary word for each sentence.

1. People only six inches tall live on the island of Lilliput in *Gulliver's Travels* by Jonathan Swift.

_____

2. A knight called Don Quixote is the hero of a book by Cervantes.

_____

3. In the play, *The Rivals* by Richard Sheridan, Mrs. Malaprop has trouble getting things straight.

_____

4. Karel Capek made up a word for machines that work for people in his play called *R.U.R.*

_____

5. In Roman mythology, Hercules does twelve impossible labors.

_____

6. Scrooge is a selfish character in *A Christmas Carol* by Charles Dickens.

_____

B. Write the letter of its literary source beside each word.

1. **jabberwocky** _____

2. **narcissus** _____

3. **utopia** _____

4. **puckish** _____

a. An impish character named Puck appears in *A Midsummer Night's Dream* by William Shakespeare.

b. Lewis Carroll created an imaginary animal called a Jabberwock in *Through the Looking-Glass*.

c. In a Greek myth, a youth named Narcissus falls in love with his own image and finally turns into a flower.

d. In 1551, Sir Thomas More wrote about Utopia, an island with a perfect social and political system.

NAME _____ DATE _____

Words From Literature

jabberwocky	lilliputian	quixotic	narcissus	robot
puckish	Herculean	utopian	scrooge	malapropism

A. Use what you know. Write the best word to complete each sentence.

1. That man doesn't like to spend his money and is sometimes called a _____ .

2. Ginnie has lots of noble but unworkable ideas; she's rather _____ .

3. In the spring, large clusters of _____ cover the fields.

4. Mom thinks it would be great to have a _____ to do the household chores.

5. This essay has no meaning; it's just _____ .

6. Henry is a fun-loving guy with a _____ smile.

7. With _____ effort, the little girl managed to carry her suitcase upstairs.

8. In a _____ , the speaker meant to say a "rude awakening," but instead blurted out a "shrewd awakening."

9. The dollhouse furniture was a _____ copy of our living room furniture.

10. Many reformers have had _____ dreams of better societies.

B. Read each question. Choose the best answer.

1. Which one suggests confusion?   ❑ malady   ❑ malapropism   ❑ malevolent

2. What does a robot do?   ❑ dream   ❑ work   ❑ think

3. Which one is an ant?   ❑ lilliputian   ❑ gargantuan   ❑ utopian

4. What kind of person is more fun?   ❑ scrooge   ❑ puckish   ❑ Herculean

 Writing to Learn

Pretend you are an author. Describe five characters in a book or play you are writing. Use at least one vocabulary word in your description of each character.

Words From Literature

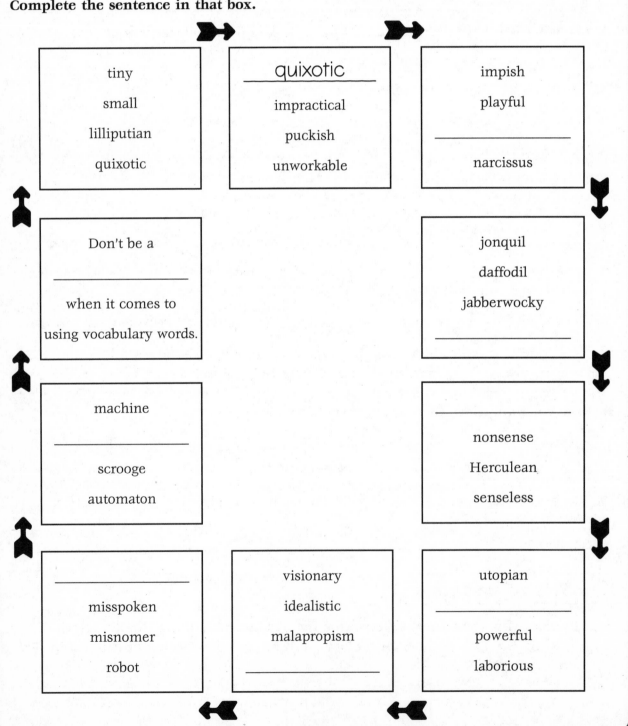

Play a game of Move On. Find a word in the first box that does *not* have the same meaning as the other three words. Move that word to the next box by writing it on the blank line. The first one is done for you. Continue until you reach the last box. Complete the sentence in that box.

tiny
small
lilliputian
quixotic

quixotic
impractical
puckish
unworkable

impish
playful
_____
narcissus

Don't be a
_____
when it comes to
using vocabulary words.

jonquil
daffodil
jabberwocky
_____

machine
_____
scrooge
automaton

_____
nonsense
Herculean
senseless

_____
misspoken
misnomer
robot

visionary
idealistic
malapropism
_____

utopian
_____
powerful
laborious

Words From Shakespeare

barefaced	monumental	majestic	dwindle	hint
radiance	castigate	frugal	gust	summit

WRITERS OFTEN MAKE UP WORDS. THESE WORDS AND 1,685 OTHERS WERE ALL INTRODUCED BY **WILLIAM SHAKESPEARE**.

If something is **barefaced**, it is without disguise.

Monumental means "large and outstanding."

Majestic means "grand or dignified."

When something **dwindles**, little remains of it.

A **hint** is an indirect suggestion.

Radiance is brilliant light.

If you **castigate** someone, you scold or punish that person.

If you are **frugal**, you spend your money carefully and sparingly.

A **gust** is a rush of wind.

The **summit** is the highest point on a mountain.

A. Read the vocabulary word. Find and circle two other words that mean almost the same thing.

1. **frugal**	generous	thrifty	sparing	fruitful
2. **castigate**	criticize	scold	castaway	praise
3. **dwindle**	enlarge	dwell	decrease	diminish
4. **barefaced**	hidden	unconcealed	barely	uncovered
5. **monumental**	stationary	lilliputian	huge	mammoth
6. **summit**	summon	peak	top	summarize
7. **majestic**	noble	imposing	magic	common
8. **gust**	squall	jest	blast	guilt

B. Write a vocabulary word for each clue.

   1. an inkling _____   **2.** brilliance _____

Words From Shakespeare

barefaced	monumental	majestic	dwindle	hint
radiance	castigate	frugal	gust	summit

A. Use what you know. Write the best word to complete each sentence.

1. The crook didn't hide the stolen goods and told a _____ lie about where he got them.

2. We were awed by the _____ of the stars on a clear night.

3. It took several days for the climbers to reach the _____ .

4. The child knew his parents would _____ him for playing ball in the house.

5. Sophie is very _____ with her allowance and saves most of it.

6. The queen looked regal and _____ in her robes and crown.

7. A _____ of wind blew the papers right out of the man's hand.

8. The bellboy gave a _____ or two about accepting a tip.

9. Workers drove carts around the airplane factory because of its _____ size.

10. After two weeks, our supplies began to _____ , so we went to a store.

B. Read each question. Choose the best answer.

1. Which one is frugal? ❑ earner ❑ saver ❑ spender

2. Which one has radiance? ❑ sun ❑ wind ❑ cloud

3. Which one has a summit? ❑ valley ❑ plateau ❑ mountain

4. What is a palace? ❑ humble ❑ majestic ❑ ordinary

 Writing to Learn

Make up a word game or puzzle using at least five vocabulary words.

NAME _____ DATE _____

Words From Shakespeare

Write the vocabulary word for each clue. Then write the circled letters on the numbered lines at the bottom of the page to answer the riddle.

WHAT IS AT THE END OF EVERYTHING?

1. not wasteful — __ __ __ __ __ __

2. intimation or allusion __ __ __ __

3. lessen __ __ __ __ __ __

4. undisguised __ __ __ __ __ __ __ __ __

5. exalted __ __ __ __ __ __ __ __

6. rebuke __ __ __ __ __ __ __

7. luminosity __ __ __ __ __ __ __ __ __ __

8. pinnacle __ __ __ __ __ __ __ __

9. a blast of wind __ __ __ __

10. enormous __ __ __ __ __ __ __ __

__ __ __ __ __ __ __ __ __ __ __
6   2   4   10 7   8   5   3   1   9

Blends

fortnight	clash	farewell	prissy	travelogue
Laundromat	flextime	motorcade	sitcom	walkathon

A **BLEND** IS A WORD FORMED WHEN PARTS OF TWO WORDS ARE COMBINED OR BLENDED TOGETHER. A BLEND IS ALSO CALLED A PORTMANTEAU WORD. A PORTMANTEAU IS A SUITCASE WITH TWO SIDES.

A **fortnight** is two weeks.

A **clash** is a loud noise.

When you say goodbye, you say **farewell**.

A **prissy** person is fussy.

An illustrated lecture about traveling is a **travelogue**.

A **Laundromat** is a commercial place for washing and drying clothes in coin-operated machines.

Flextime is an arrangement workers make with employers to set their own work schedules.

If you ride in a **motorcade**, you are in a procession of cars.

A walking marathon is a **walkathon**.

A **sitcom** is a humorous television show.

A. Write the blend formed from each pair of words.

1. situation and comedy   _____

2. fourteen and night   _____

3. walk and marathon   _____

4. prim and sissy   _____

5. motor and cavalcade   _____

6. travel and monologue   _____

7. flexible and time   _____

8. fare and well   _____

B. Write the vocabulary word for each clue.

1. a harsh sound _____   2. a place for dirty clothes _____

Blends

fortnight	clash	farewell	prissy	travelogue
Laundromat	flextime	motorcade	sitcom	walkathon

A. Use what you know. Write the best word to complete each sentence.

1. The cookie tin made a loud _____ when it fell to the tile floor.

2. Iris giggles when she watches that _____ on Wednesday nights.

3. We took part in a _____ to help raise money for a good cause.

4. Mr. Tingley works _____ hours so he can be home when Jim's school is out.

5. It was hard to say _____ when our visit was over.

6. Barry took two bags of clothing to the _____ .

7. The students saw a _____ about an expedition on the Amazon River.

8. The President's _____ moved slowly down the boulevard.

9. My bean seeds sprouted in less than a _____ .

10. The little girl was rather _____ and didn't want to get her hands dirty.

B. Read each question. Choose the best answer.

1. Which one is good exercise?   ❏ walkout   ❏ walkway   ❏ walkathon

2. Which one is the longest?   ❏ weekend   ❏ weeknight   ❏ fortnight

3. What is a sitcom?   ❏ comedy   ❏ tragedy   ❏ history

4. What's in a Laundromat?   ❏ computer   ❏ dishwasher   ❏ dryer

Writing to Learn

Describe a scene for a sitcom. Use at least four vocabulary words.

NAME _____   DATE _____

Blends

An analogy is a comparison based on how things are related to one another. Complete each of these analogies with a vocabulary word.

1. A nursery is to a florist as a cleaner is to a _____ .

2. Hot is to cold as hello is to _____ .

3. A dancer is to a ballet as an actor is to a _____ .

4. Pleasant is to antagonistic as carefree is to _____ .

5. A flatcar is to a train as a limousine is to a _____ .

6. Siren is to wail as cymbal is to _____ .

7. A half hour is to an hour as a _____ is to a month.

8. A commercial is to an infomercial as a _____ is to a documentary.

9. A biathlon is to a triathlon as a _____ is to a marathon.

10. Commission is to payment as _____ is to employment.

NAME _____   DATE _____

Content Words: Weather

blustery	humid	stratus	inversion	precipitation
typhoon	cirrus	cumulus	monsoon	meteorologist

▍SPECIAL WORDS NAME DIFFERENT
ASPECTS OF **WEATHER**.

A **meteorologist** studies atmospheric conditions and forecasts the weather.

When it is **blustery**, the wind is noisy and stormy.

Humid means "moist or slightly wet."

A **stratus** cloud is low and gray and often brings rain or snow.

An **inversion** is when air temperature increases at high altitudes instead of decreasing as it normally does.

Precipitation is rain, snow, sleet, or hail.

A **typhoon** is a violent cyclone or hurricane in the western Pacific Ocean.

A **cirrus** cloud is high and thin and means fair weather.

A **cumulus** cloud is puffy and means fair weather.

A **monsoon** is a seasonal wind that usually brings heavy rains.

A. Write a word or phrase from the box to go with each vocabulary word.

shower	wet wind	tempest
gusty	damp air	reversal of air temperature

1. **typhoon** _____   2. **monsoon** _____

3. **humid** _____   4. **inversion** _____

5. **blustery** _____   6. **precipitation** _____

B. Write the vocabulary word for each picture.

1. _____   2. _____

3. _____   4. _____

NAME _____ DATE _____

Content Words: Weather

blustery	humid	stratus	inversion	precipitation
typhoon	cirrus	cumulus	monsoon	meteorologist

A. Use what you know. Write the best word to complete each sentence.

1. Martina listened to the radio to hear what the _____ said about the weather.

2. The low, gray _____ clouds looked threatening.

3. The wet, _____ air made it harder for the participants in the walkathon.

4. High in the sky, we could see thin _____ clouds.

5. A _____ is similar to a hurricane and can cause great damage.

6. The wind was so _____ that small branches broke off the trees.

7. The _____ blows from the southwest from April to October, bringing heavy rains to parts of Asia.

8. As we drove up the mountain, we noticed that an _____ had caused the temperature to rise.

9. Bart wore his trench coat in case there was any _____ later in the day.

10. It was a lovely afternoon with fluffy _____ clouds floating overhead.

B. Read each question. Choose the best answer.

1. What do you need for precipitation?　❒ sunglasses　❒ umbrella　❒ sandals

2. Which one looks like cotton?　❒ stratus　❒ cumulus　❒ nimbus

3. What does a meteorologist do?　❒ prevent　❒ predict　❒ presume

4. What is humid air?　❒ chilly　❒ wet　❒ dry

✏ Writing to Learn

Pretend you are a meteorologist. Write a weather report. Use at least four vocabulary words.

Content Words: Weather

Use the vocabulary words to fill in the map. Then add other weather words that you know.

Clouds

1. _____

2. _____

3. _____

Winds and Storms

4. _____

5. _____

6. _____

Weather Words

People

7. _____

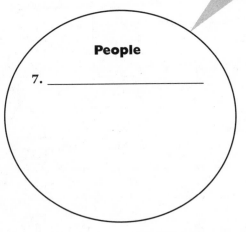

Other

8. _____

9. _____

10. _____

Content Words: Music

aria	clef	staccato	tempo	adagio
percussion	crescendo	overture	chord	allegro

SPECIAL WORDS NAME DIFFERENT
THINGS IN **MUSIC**.

A **clef** shows the pitch of musical notes.

Music with breaks between tones is played in a
staccato manner.

Tempo is the time or speed in which music is played.

Adagio means in "a slow tempo."

Percussion instruments make sounds when they are struck.

Crescendo is an increase in volume or intensity.

An **overture** introduces a musical work such as an opera.

A **chord** is three or more tones sounded together.

Allegro means "in a fast tempo."

An **aria** is a song for
one voice or instrument.

A. Write a word from the box to go with each vocabulary word.

drum	introduction	interrupted
moderate	rapid	melody

1. **allegro** _____

2. **percussion** _____

3. **staccato** _____

4. **overture** _____

5. **adagio** _____

6. **aria** _____

B. Draw a line from each word to the phrase that tells about it.

1. **tempo**   a. rising sound

2. **clef**   b. sound together in harmony

3. **chord**   c. musical mark

4. **crescendo**   d. time pattern

Content Words: Music

| aria | clef | staccato | tempo | adagio |
| percussion | crescendo | overture | chord | allegro |

A. Use what you know. Write the best word to complete each sentence.

1. An _____ gives a preview of the musical themes that will follow.

2. Her voice rose in a _____ as the song ended.

3. The band struck up a lively _____ as the parade began.

4. The audience applauded after the singer's beautiful _____ .

5. The dancers moved in rapid steps to the _____ tempo.

6. A snare drum is an example of a _____ instrument.

7. This sheet music is marked with a G _____ .

8. This piece is played in a slow _____ tempo.

9. The dripping rain made a _____ sound as it plopped on the windowsill.

10. The pianist played several _____ as the violins tuned up.

B. Read each question. Choose the best answer.

1. Which one is for a singer? ❒ area ❒ arctic ❒ aria

2. What's an overture? ❒ ending ❒ encore ❒ beginning

3. Which one's percussion? ❒ clarinet ❒ viola ❒ cymbals

4. What's a crescendo? ❒ decrease ❒ level ❒ increase

🎵 Writing to Learn

Write the copy for a CD package. Use at least five vocabulary words.

Content Words: Music

Use the clues to complete the puzzle.

Across

3. marimbas are an example
6. disconnected music
9. quick time
10. musical prelude

Down

1. musical sign
2. song for one
4. on the rise
5. unhurried pace
7. tones together
8. musical speed

Latin Roots *aud, grat, ject*

audible	auditorium	congratulate	gratify	reject
audition	audience	gratitude	inject	conjecture

MANY WORDS HAVE LATIN ROOTS.

Something that is **audible** can be heard.

Root:

Aud means "hear."   An **audition** is a hearing to hire a performer.

An **auditorium** is a large space for an audience.

People gathered in a place to see or hear something make up an **audience**.

Grat means "pleasing."   When you **congratulate** someone, you express good wishes.

Gratitude is thankfulness.

Gratify means "to please."

Ject means "throw."   **Inject** means "to fill or insert."

If you **reject** something, you refuse it.

When you **conjecture**, you make a guess.

A. Read the vocabulary word. Find and circle two other words that mean almost the same thing.

1. **gratify**	delight	fulfill	gravity
2. **conjecture**	conjunction	surmise	suppose
3. **inject**	introduce	insert	expect
4. **reject**	repudiate	accept	discard
5. **gratitude**	appreciation	grasping	gratefulness
6. **audition**	radiance	presentation	hearing
7. **congratulate**	compliment	praise	lament

B. Write a vocabulary word for each clue.

1. large room found in schools and other public places _____

2. group of people who attend a performance _____

3. noise within earshot _____

Latin Roots *aud, grat, ject*

audible	auditorium	congratulate	gratify	reject
audition	audience	gratitude	inject	conjecture

A. Use what you know. Write the best word to complete each sentence.

1. Gabriella had an _____ for a role in the school play.

2. Our cat is fussy and will _____ any food she doesn't like.

3. Emma is very shy and speaks in a barely _____ voice.

4. The stories in that newspaper show that the reporters _____ better than they research.

5. As the musicians took a bow, people in the _____ rose to their feet and clapped.

6. The hostess tried to _____ some fun into the party.

7. The neighbors were full of _____ when we rescued their dog.

8. If you must _____ your hunger, eat some fruit.

9. All the students filed into the _____ to hear the principal speak.

10. My aunt called to _____ me for winning a prize in math.

B. Read each question. Choose the best answer.

1. Which one's a test?   ❑ audition   ❑ auditorium   ❑ auction

2. What do you show at Thanksgiving?   ❑ conjecture   ❑ gratitude   ❑ displeasure

3. Which fruit do you reject?   ❑ fresh   ❑ ripe   ❑ rotten

4. Whom might you congratulate?   ❑ loser   ❑ graduate   ❑ victim

✍ Writing to Learn

Explain why it is helpful to learn the root of a word. Use at least three vocabulary words as your examples.

Latin Roots *aud, grat, ject*

Read the clues. Write the word next to the clue. Then find and circle each word in the puzzle.

1. satisfy   _____

2. deny   _____

3. hearable   _____

4. insert   _____

5. spectators   _____

6. theater   _____

7. tryout   _____

8. extend best wishes   _____

9. theorize or conclude   _____

10. thankfulness   _____

```
C  O  N  G  R  A  T  U  L  A  T  E  D
O  B  J  R  K  Q  C  F  D  X  R  T  K
N  E  G  A  O  Z  L  V  P  H  L  M  C
J  S  Y  T  L  A  U  D  I  T  I  O  N
E  N  H  I  W  S  D  K  N  U  C  J  R
C  P  Z  T  O  Q  M  X  J  E  U  E  A
T  E  A  U  D  I  B  L  E  P  G  X  W
U  T  C  D  S  N  V  L  C  R  R  N  I
R  E  J  E  C  T  A  U  T  I  A  Q  L
E  X  F  N  P  W  B  F  Y  G  T  M  H
V  E  Y  A  U  D  I  T  O  R  I  U  M
T  Q  N  K  H  Z  D  N  J  Z  F  L  O
A  U  D  I  E  N  C  E  W  S  Y  M  B
```

Greek Word Parts *aero, belli, pan*

aerobics	**aerial**	**aerate**	**belligerent**	**pandemonium**
aerodynamics	**aeronautics**	**rebellion**	**panacea**	**panorama**

▌ MANY ENGLISH WORDS HAVE **GREEK** WORD PARTS.

The design and construction of aircraft is called **aeronautics**.

Root:

Aero means "air."   **Aerobics** is a system of exercises that promote fitness.

Aerodynamics is the branch of physics related to the motion of air and other gases.

An **aerial** is a wire or rod used in sending out and receiving electromagnetic waves.

When you **aerate** something, you expose and mix it with air or other gases.

Belli means "war."   A **rebellion** is an uprising.

Belligerent means "aggressive or warlike."

Pan means "all."   A **panacea** is a cure for all problems.

Pandemonium is a noisy uproar.

A **panorama** is an unlimited view over a wide area.

A. Read the words in each row. Write a vocabulary word that means almost the same thing.

1. revolt, insurrection _____

2. remedy, correction _____

3. combative, quarrelsome _____

4. turmoil, noise _____

5. vista, outlook _____

6. vaporize, oxygenize _____

7. aviation, flying _____

8. antenna, receiver _____

B. Underline the Greek word part in each word.

1. **aerodynamics**

2. **aerobics**

NAME _____ DATE _____

Greek Word Parts *aero, belli, pan*

aerobics	aerial	aerate	belligerent	pandemonium
aerodynamics	aeronautics	rebellion	panacea	panorama

A. Use what you know. Write the best word to complete each sentence.

1. The _____ from the mountaintop was breathtaking.

2. The passenger on the bus had a _____ attitude and would not move over.

3. Doreen takes an _____ class at the health club on Mondays.

4. When the excited puppies got loose, there was _____ in the house.

5. Without an _____ , our TV reception was poor.

6. Money is not a _____ for all your troubles.

7. Dr. Robart works in the field of _____ and studies how forces act on objects moving through air.

8. The newscaster reported that soldiers put down a _____ in a small foreign country.

9. To make soda water, _____ regular water with carbon dioxide.

10. John attends _____ school to learn about aviation.

B. Read each question. Choose the best answer.

1. Where might there be a panorama? ❏ closet ❏ roof ❏ tunnel

2. Where might you do aerobics? ❏ gym ❏ library ❏ bakery

3. What causes people to be belligerent? ❏ peace ❏ happiness ❏ anger

4. What's pandemonium like? ❏ confusion ❏ quiet ❏ orderly

 **Writing to Learn**

Explain how three of the vocabulary words are formed.

Greek Word Parts *aero, belli, pan*

Read each list of words. Write a vocabulary word to go with each group.

1.   solution

     cure

     remedy

     _____

2.   mutiny

     uprising

     riot

     _____

3.   pugnacious

     aggressive

     combative

     _____

4.   view

     survey

     landscape

     _____

5.   wire

     rod

     electromagnetic waves

     _____

6.   physics

     forces

     gases

     _____

7.   disorder

     chaos

     uproar

     _____

8.   exercise

     oxygen

     energy

     _____

9.   flying

     aircraft

     aviation

     _____

10.   mineral water

     mix

     air

     _____

Greek Word Parts *chronos, phon*

anachronism	chronicle	synchronize	cacophony	phonics
chronic	chronology	megaphone	euphonious	symphony

▌MANY ENGLISH WORDS HAVE
GREEK WORD PARTS.

Cacophony is a harsh, clashing sound.

Root:

Chronos means "time."

In an **anachronism**, an event or object is placed in a time period where it doesn't belong.

Chronic means "lasting a long time."

A **chronicle** is a record of happenings.

A **chronology** is a list of events arranged in the order in which they occurred.

Synchronize means "to happen at the same time."

Phon means "sound."

A **megaphone** is a horn that increases the loudness of a voice.

Euphonious means "pleasing to the ear."

Phonics is the association of letters with speech sounds.

A **symphony** is a composition for an orchestra to play.

A. Draw a line to match each description to the correct vocabulary word.

1. an account   a. **cacophony**

2. used by cheerleaders   b. **chronicle**

3. coincide   c. **megaphone**

4. musical piece   d. **euphonious**

5. harmonious   e. **chronic**

6. continuous   f. **synchronize**

7. dissonance   g. **symphony**

B. Underline the Greek word part in each word.

1. **phonics**

2. **chronology**

3. **anachronism**

NAME _____ DATE _____

Greek Word Parts *chronos, phon*

anachronism	chronicle	synchronize	cacophony	phonics
chronic	chronology	megaphone	euphonious	symphony

A. Use what you know. Write the best word to complete each sentence.

1. The detective reconstructed the _____ of events leading to the crime.

2. Those bells make a beautiful, _____ sound in the wind.

3. The conductor raised his baton to begin the _____ .

4. That picture of a car in the 1600s is an _____ because there were no cars then.

5. Ned yelled at the crowd through his _____ as the team took the field.

6. Let's _____ our watches so we arrive at the same time.

7. The boy suffers from a _____ illness and is often absent.

8. The clatter of dishes, voices, and phones creates a _____ of sound in the kitchen.

9. The children learned _____ as part of their reading lesson.

10. Our class read a _____ of our town at the historical museum.

B. Read each question. Choose the best answer.

1. Which one is an error? ❏ analogy   ❏ anachronism   ❏ anagram

2. Which one amplifies? ❏ megalopolis   ❏ megawatt   ❏ megaphone

3. Which one is euphonious? ❏ scream   ❏ screech   ❏ birdsong

4. Which one plays a symphony? ❏ band   ❏ orchestra   ❏ quartet

✏ Writing to Learn

Write a chronicle about a day in school. Use at least four vocabulary words.

© 240 VOCABULARY WORDS FOR GRADE 6   SCHOLASTIC PROFESSIONAL BOOKS

Greek Word Parts *chronos, phon*

Play Tic-Tac-Synonym. Read each word. Then draw a line through three words in the box that are synonyms for that word. Your line can be vertical, horizontal, or diagonal.

1. synchronize

clockwise	swim	differ
synthetic	phonetic	delegate
correspond	match	coincide

2. cacophony

cackle	cracker	babel
sweet	symphony	discordant
practical	defiant	jarring

3. chronic

staggered	ongoing	sonic
irregular	persistent	sickly
unpleasant	unremitting	terminate

4. euphonious

shattering	phony	melodious
chronological	sincere	tuneful
lonely	ridiculous	harmonious

5. chronicle

complain	everlasting	narrative
exaggerate	account	container
record	crystal	careful

British English

braces	torch	lorry	petrol	cinema
diversion	crumpet	dustbin	chips	mackintosh

▎SOME ENGLISH WORDS HAVE DIFFERENT MEANINGS IN
BRITAIN THAN THEY DO IN THE UNITED STATES.

If you wear **braces**, you have on suspenders.

A **torch** is a flashlight.

Petrol is gas.

If you go to the **cinema**, you go to the movies.

A **diversion** is a detour.

A **crumpet** is a muffin.

When you throw something in a trash can, you put it in a **dustbin**.

In Britain, French fries are called **chips**.

A **mackintosh** is a raincoat.

A **lorry** is a truck.

A. Write a vocabulary word for each picture.

1.   _____

2. _____

3. _____

4. _____

5. _____

6. _____

B. Write a vocabulary word for each clue.

1. carries freight _____   2. made from potatoes _____

3. a kind of bread _____   4. film _____

NAME _____ DATE _____

British English

braces	torch	lorry	petrol	cinema
diversion	crumpet	dustbin	chips	mackintosh

A. Use what you know. Write the best word to complete each sentence.

1. A popular English meal is fish and _____ .

2. Mr. Browning hooked a thumb through his blue and gold _____ .

3. If it's raining, put on your new _____ .

4. The _____ pulled up to the loading dock at the store.

5. We went to the _____ last night and saw my favorite actor.

6. Be sure to put _____ in the car before we leave for our trip.

7. Luckily, Althea had a _____ when the electricity failed.

8. Our ride took longer than usual because of the _____ .

9. Mrs. Blake toasted a _____ to have with her tea.

10. Cyrus crumpled up the paper and tossed it into the _____ .

B. Read each question. Choose the best answer.

1. Which one causes delays? ❏ direction ❏ diversion ❏ division

2. Which one's a fuel? ❏ petrol ❏ torch ❏ petrel

3. Which one's a carrier? ❏ loft ❏ lorry ❏ lotus

4. What are braces for? ❏ socks ❏ vest ❏ pants

Writing to Learn

Write an e-mail message from a British pen pal to one in the United States. Use at least four vocabulary words.

British English

Complete the chart with the British and American words for each definition.

Definition	British Word	American Word
1. outer garment for rain		
2. motion picture		
3. accessory that holds up trousers		
4. fuel for automobiles		
5. battery-operated light		
6. alternate route		
7. container for litter		
8. round, flat cake		
9. thin pieces of potato fried in fat		
10. large vehicle for transporting things		

Word Stories

tantalize	boulevard	poinsettia	mercurial	coward
tulle	nucleus	flamingo	blazer	magnolia

❚ MANY WORDS HAVE INTERESTING **STORIES** ABOUT THEIR ORIGINS.

If you **tantalize** someone, you torment that person.

A **boulevard** is a wide avenue.

Someone who is **mercurial** is quick and changeable.

A **coward** is someone who lacks courage.

Tulle is a fine net used in veils and women's clothes.

A **nucleus** is the core of a cell and controls its growth.

A **flamingo** is a large bird with bright pink feathers.

A **blazer** is a type of jacket. / A **magnolia** is a kind of tree with large flowers.

A **poinsettia** is a plant often used as a holiday decoration.

A. Write a vocabulary word for each word story.

1. Sailors aboard the British ship *Blazer* wore a new kind of coat. _____

2. Long ago in France, the tops of ramparts called *bolouarts* were used as places to walk. _____

3. Coart was a timid hare in an old French fable about Reynard the Fox. _____

4. The Latin word *nux* means "kernel." _____

5. A fine open-meshed silk was first made in Tulle, France. _____

6. The Latin word *flamma* means flame. _____

B. Draw a line from each vocabulary word to the person associated with the word.

1. magnolia   **a.** The Roman god Mercury was known for speed.

2. mercurial   **b.** J.R. Poinsett, a U.S. ambassador to Mexico, brought a plant with him when he returned to his homeland.

3. poinsettia   **c.** Tantalus, a Greek god, was punished in an unusual way.

4. tantalize   **d.** Pierre Magnol was a French botanist.

Word Stories

tantalize	boulevard	poinsettia	mercurial	coward
tulle	nucleus	flamingo	blazer	magnolia

A. Use what you know. Write the best word to complete each sentence.

1. The city of Paris is known for its wide _____ .

2. The fantastic _____ is a southern bird with a long neck and legs.

3. Muriel didn't want the others to think she was a _____ , so she walked across the rope bridge.

4. Every once in a while, a breeze would _____ us with the promise of cool air during the heat wave.

5. The ballerina wore a tutu with a _____ skirt.

6. In the spring, the blossoms on a _____ tree perfume the air.

7. Zack wasn't entirely comfortable with Andrew because of his _____ temperament.

8. Many of the men at the summer party wore blue _____ .

9. Without a _____ , a cell cannot divide.

10. Every Christmas, florists sell hundreds of red _____ plants.

B. Read each question. Choose the best answer.

1. Which one has wings?   ❑ flamingo   ❑ flamenco   ❑ flannel

2. What might a boulevard have?   ❑ turret   ❑ tulle   ❑ traffic

3. Which one has sleeves?   ❑ vest   ❑ leotard   ❑ blazer

4. What might a coward do?   ❑ hide   ❑ fight   ❑ attack

✎ Writing to Learn

Find out more about the story behind two of the vocabulary words.
Write a report about the words.

Word Stories

Play a game of Move On. Find a word in the first box that does not go with the
other three words. Move that word to the next box by writing it on the blank line.
Continue until you reach the last box. Complete the sentence in that box.

biology

cell

blazer

nucleus

_____

coat

jacket

tulle

fabric

_____

veil

tantalize

No one will call you a

_____

if you do the

right thing.

tease

vex

_____

mercurial

houseplant

holiday

_____

coward

fickle

animated

magnolia

_____

promenade

avenue

_____

poinsettia

_____

flaming

avian

boulevard

tree

_____

blossom

flamingo

Funny Words

hootenanny	snaggletooth	skedaddle	topsy-turvy	gewgaw
balderdash	flummox	wishy-washy	thingamabob	hunky-dory

SOME WORDS ARE FUN TO KNOW AND USE BECAUSE THEY ARE COLORFUL AND FUNNY.

A **hootenanny** is a gathering of folksingers.

When you **skedaddle**, you run away suddenly.

Topsy-turvy means "upside down."

A **gewgaw** is a showy trinket.

Balderdash means "nonsense."

If you **flummox** someone, you bewilder that person.

If something is **wishy-washy**, it is weak.

If you can't think of the name for something, you might say it's a **thingamabob**.

Hunky dory means "okay."

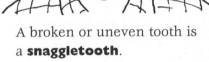

A broken or uneven tooth is a **snaggletooth**.

A. Read the words in each row. Cross out the word that does not have a similar meaning to the vocabulary word.

1. **flummox**	flutter	confuse	confound
2. **gewgaw**	doodad	knickknack	guffaw
3. **wishy-washy**	clean	feeble	insipid
4. **balderdash**	poppycock	fiddlesticks	hairless
5. **skedaddle**	doubt	depart	leave
6. **topsy-turvy**	disorderly	chaotic	calm
7. **thingamabob**	ungrammatical	doohickey	whatchamacallit

B. Write a vocabulary word for each clue.

1. a dental problem   2. not to worry   3. a jam session

_____   _____   _____

Funny Words

hootenanny	snaggletooth	skedaddle	topsy-turvy	gewgaw
balderdash	flummox	wishy-washy	thingamabob	hunky-dory

A. Use what you know. Write the best word to complete each sentence.

1. The tourists stopped to look at a _____ in the window of a souvenir shop.

2. After the match, the boxer had a _____ and went to the dentist.

3. It was a lazy, warm day, and we all felt kind of _____ about making plans.

4. When the waiter dropped the tray, the dishes went _____ all over the place.

5. Each summer, fiddle players and singers come from all over to the _____ .

6. "Don't worry, everything is _____ ," Uncle Ike assured us after the storm.

7. That statement is nonsense and _____ .

8. "Quick! Get me the _____ !" yelled Frank in excitement when the shelf fell.

9. The boys decided to _____ before their mother thought of any more chores.

10. "Don't let the big words in this book _____ you," said the librarian.

B. Read each question. Choose the best answer.

1. What might be a gewgaw? ❑ pin ❑ book ❑ couch

2. Which one's an event? ❑ snaggletooth ❑ hootenanny ❑ hunky dory

3. Who might be wishy-washy? ❑ coward ❑ villain ❑ heroine

4. How might you react to a storm? ❑ sleep ❑ dillydally ❑ skedaddle

✎ Writing to Learn

Write a promotional piece describing a hootenanny. Use at least three vocabulary words.

Funny Words

Read the clues. Then complete the puzzle.

1. perplex

2. all right

3. a folksingers' happening

4. jagged protrusion from the mouth

5. gutless

6. a bauble

7. a what's-its-name

8. in disarray

9. flee

10. foolishness

1. **F** __ __ __ __ __ __

2. __ **U** __ __ __ - __ __ __ __

3. __ __ __ __ **N** __ __ __

4. __ **N** __ __ __ __ __ __ __ __ __

5. __ __ __ __ **Y** - __ __ __ __ __

6. __ __ **W** __ __ __

7. __ __ __ __ __ __ __ __ **O** __

8. __ __ __ __ __ - __ __ **R** __ __

9. __ __ __ __ **D** __ __ __ __

10. __ __ __ __ __ __ __ __ **S** __

NAME _____   DATE _____

Confusing Words

tortuous	**plaintiff**	**insinuate**	**desolate**	**ally**
torturous	**plaintive**	**incinerate**	**dissolute**	**alley**

▌ SOME WORDS ARE **CONFUSING** BECAUSE THEY LOOK AND/OR SOUND MUCH LIKE OTHER WORDS.

Tortuous means "winding."

Something that is **torturous** causes great pain.

A person who begins a lawsuit is a **plaintiff**.

Plaintive means "sad."

Insinuate means "to suggest in an indirect way."

If you **incinerate** something, you burn it.

Dissolute means "immoral."

An **ally** is a supporter.

An **alley** is a narrow street.

Desolate means "deserted."

A. Read the words in each row. Write a vocabulary word that means almost the same thing.

1. hint, imply   _____

2. lane, path   _____

3. twisting, serpentine   _____

4. barren, uninhabited   _____

5. lewd, dissipated   _____

6. anguished, miserable   _____

7. associate, confederate   _____

8. mournful, melancholy   _____

B. Write a vocabulary word for each clue.

1. cause a flame _____   **2.** an accuser _____

NAME _____   DATE _____

Confusing Words

tortuous	plaintiff	insinuate	desolate	ally
torturous	plaintive	incinerate	dissolute	alley

A. Use what you know. Write the best word to complete each sentence.

1. In the hours just before dawn, the streets are empty and _____ .

2. The _____ road zigzagged up the mountain.

3. In this building, the city _____ its trash.

4. Britain is an important _____ of the United States.

5. The _____ story made Melvina want to cry.

6. Did Zena _____ that your dress is out of style?

7. The people on this street park their cars in an _____ behind their houses.

8. Getting into the cold ocean water is _____ for some beachgoers.

9. In this film, Connie plays a wayward character who is very _____ .

10. Our neighbor is a _____ in a civil law case about his fence.

B. Read each question. Choose the best answer.

1. Which one can you count on?   ❏ alley   ❏ ally   ❏ allée

2. Which one can't be tortuous?   ❏ airstrip   ❏ trail   ❏ river

3. How might a lost hiker feel?   ❏ desolate   ❏ dissolute   ❏ dissolved

4. What can be plaintive?   ❏ food   ❏ song   ❏ shoes

✍ Writing to Learn

Write a science fiction story. Use at least four vocabulary words.

NAME _____   DATE _____

Confusing Words

Use the clues to complete the puzzle.

Across

1. sorrowful
5. passageway
6. cremate
7. circuitous
8. debauched
9. lonely

Down

1. a complainant
2. affiliate
3. suggest
4. distressing

Prefixes *de-, fore-, im-, micro-, anti-*

devalue	foreshadow	improper	microcosm	antitoxin
desegregate	foresight	improvident	microscope	antisocial

▌A **PREFIX** IS A WORD PART THAT IS ADDED TO THE
BEGINNING OF A WORD AND CHANGES ITS MEANING.

de- means "down" or "away from"
fore- means "in front of"
im- means "not"
micro- means "small"
anti- means "against"

A **microscope** is an
instrument that makes
small things look larger.

Devalue means "to reduce the value of something."

Desegregate means "to end segregation."

If you **foreshadow** something, you indicate it beforehand.

Foresight is wisdom. / **Improper** means "not according to standards."

Improvident means "not careful in providing for the future."

A **microcosm** is a little world. / An **antitoxin** makes the body safe from disease.

If you are **antisocial**, you are not sociable.

A. Read the words in each row. Circle the word that means almost the same thing as the vocabulary word.

1. **foresight**	forego	wisdom	foreground
2. **improvident**	imprudent	interesting	immigrate
3. **antisocial**	antecedent	gregarious	unfriendly
4. **improper**	improbable	unseemly	impulsive
5. **devalue**	increase	deregulate	lower
6. **foreshadow**	presage	foreshorten	forgive

B. Add the correct prefix to each word to form a new word. Use the meaning clue in parentheses to help you.

1. (away from) _____ segregate   2. (small) _____ scope

3. (small) _____ cosm   4. (against) _____ toxin

NAME _____ DATE _____

Prefixes *de-, fore-, im-, micro-, anti-*

devalue	**foreshadow**	**improper**	**microcosm**	**antitoxin**
desegregate	**foresight**	**improvident**	**microscope**	**antisocial**

A. Use what you know. Write the best word to complete each sentence.

1. Grandma says it is _____ to wear a baseball cap at dinner.

2. A law was passed to _____ the nation's schools.

3. Often, an author will _____ an event by bringing it up earlier in the story.

4. A hermit is usually an _____ person who prefers to be alone.

5. The young man was _____ with his money and didn't worry about the future.

6. Dad had the _____ to keep a first aid kit in the car.

7. That fish tank is a _____ of the ocean.

8. The government will _____ the exchange rate of currency next week.

9. This serum contains an _____ for diphtheria.

10. The students studied slides under a _____ .

B. Read each question. Choose the best answer.

1. What is spitting? ❏ improvident ❏ improper ❏ improvement

2. Which shows foresight? ❏ forgetting ❏ worrying ❏ planning

3. Which one's a literary term? ❏ foreshadow ❏ antisocial ❏ microcosm

4. Which one's improvident? ❏ spendthrift ❏ earner ❏ saver

✎ Writing to Learn

Explain how a prefix changes the meaning of a word. Use at least four vocabulary words as examples.

Prefixes *de-, fore-, im-, micro-, anti-*

Underline the prefix in each word below. Use what you know about the prefix meaning to write the meaning of the word. Check your answers in a dictionary.

1. antimissile _____

_____

2. decompress _____

_____

3. foretell _____

_____

4. antipathy _____

_____

5. microfilm _____

_____

6. forerunner _____

_____

7. immovable _____

_____

8. immeasurable _____

_____

9. defrost _____

_____

10. microphone _____

_____

Suffixes *-ance, -ity, -al, -less, -ible*

tolerance	**velocity**	**sensational**	**remorseless**	**convertible**
arrogance	**hospitality**	**stoical**	**defenseless**	**irreversible**

A **SUFFIX** IS A WORD PART THAT IS ADDED TO THE END OF A WORD AND CHANGES THE WORD'S MEANING.

-ance and *-ity* mean "state of being"
-al means "relating to"
-less means "lack of"
-ible means "can be"

I convert to a topless car.

A **convertible** is something that can be changed.

Tolerance is respect for others.

Arrogance is pride.

Velocity is speed. / **Hospitality** is a warm welcome for guests.

If something is **sensational**, it is outstanding. / **Stoical** means "indifferent to pleasure or pain."

When someone is **remorseless**, that person has no pity.

If you are **defenseless**, you have no way of protecting yourself.

Irreversible means "unable to be changed."

A. Read the words in each row. Write a vocabulary word that means almost the same thing.

1. impassive, unaffected   _____

2. merciless, pitiless   _____

3. haughtiness, self-importance   _____

4. rapidity, swiftness   _____

5. spectacular, exciting   _____

6. vulnerable, helpless   _____

7. consideration, forbearance   _____

8. permanent, unalterable   _____

B. Underline the suffix in each word.

1. **convertible**   2. **hospitality**

Suffixes -ance, -ity, -al, -less, -ible

tolerance	velocity	sensational	remorseless	convertible
arrogance	hospitality	stoical	defenseless	irreversible

A. Use what you know. Write the best word to complete each sentence.

1. The instructor was _____ and kept the class working despite the heat.

2. We were amazed at the _____ of the puck as it flew over the ice.

3. A goal in our school is to practice _____ for all.

4. Bonnie thanked her hosts for their kind _____ .

5. Jackie chased the cat away from the _____ baby bird.

6. The damage from the flood is extensive and _____ in some places.

7. The acrobats in the circus really put on a _____ show.

8. Despite her injury, Verna was _____ about the pain.

9. The occupants of the _____ stopped to put the top down.

10. Donna thought the guide showed great _____ toward the people who weren't familiar with art.

B. Read each question. Choose the best answer.

1. Where could you find hospitality?   ❐ inn   ❐ theater   ❐ garage

2. What's a top hit?   ❐ stoical   ❐ sensational   ❐ remorseless

3. Which one has wheels?   ❐ conversion   ❐ convertible   ❐ convert

4. Which one's defenseless?   ❐ soldier   ❐ marine   ❐ infant

Writing to Learn

Explain how a suffix changes the meaning of a word. Use at least four vocabulary words as examples.

NAME _____ DATE _____

Suffixes -ance, -ity, -al, -less, -ible

Here's a challenge for you. Write at least four words that end in each suffix. Use one of the words from each group in a sentence.

1. _____

  _____   *-ance*   _____

  _____   _____

  _____

2. _____

  _____   *-ible*   _____

  _____   _____

  _____

3. _____

  _____   *-ity*   _____

  _____   _____

  _____

4. _____

  _____   *-al*   _____

  _____   _____

  _____

5. _____

  _____   *-less*   _____

  _____   _____

  _____

Word List

abundant, p. 9
adagio, p. 48
aerate, p.54
aerial, p. 54
aerobics, p. 54
aerodynamics, p. 54
aeronautics, p. 54
afghan, p. 30
algebra, p. 33
allegro, p. 48
alley, p. 69
ally, p. 69
anachronism, p. 57
ancestors, p. 15
antisocial, p. 72
antitoxin, p. 72
aria, p. 48
arrogance, p. 75
atoll, p. 30
audible, p. 51
audience, p. 51
audition, p. 51
auditorium, p. 51

bacitracin, p. 27
badminton, p. 30
balderdash, p. 66
barefaced, p. 39
belligerent, p. 54
blazer, p. 63
blustery, p. 45
boulevard, p. 63
boycott, p. 27
braces, p. 60
buffet, p. 24
buffet, p. 24

cacophony, p. 57
canary, p. 30
cardigan, p. 27
cashmere, p. 30
castigate, p. 39
chips, p. 60
chord, p. 48
chronic, p. 57
chronicle, p. 57
chronology, p. 57
cinema, p. 60
cirrus, p. 45
clash, p. 42
clef, p. 48
commotion, p. 6
congenial, p. 12
congratulate, p. 51
conjecture, p. 51
consolidate, p. 6

convertible, p. 75
coward, p. 63
crescendo, p. 48
crumpet, p. 60
cumulus, p. 45
currants, p. 30

defenseless, p. 75
denim, p. 30
derrick, p. 27
desegregate, p. 72
desolate, p. 69
destiny, p. 6
devalue, p. 72
disagreeable, p. 12
disciple, p. 9
disrespect, p. 15
dissolute, p. 69
diversion, p. 60
drive-in, p. 18
dustbin, p. 60
dwindle, p. 39

entice, p. 12
euphonious, p. 57

factual, p. 12
fanciful, p. 12
farewell, p. 42
flamingo, p. 63
flextime, p. 42
flummox, p. 66
foreshadow, p. 72
foresight, p. 72
fortnight, p. 42
frolic, p. 33
frugal, p. 39

getaway, p. 18
gewgaw, p. 66
glum, p. 6
gratify, p. 51
gratitude, p. 51
gregarious, p. 6
gust, p. 39

haggard, p. 9
haughty, p. 6
health club, p. 18
Herculean, p. 36
hew, p. 21
high rise, p. 18
hint, p. 39
hootenanny, p. 66
hospitality, p. 75
hostel, p. 21
hostile, p. 21

hue, p. 21
humid, p. 45
hunky dory, p. 66

iceberg, p. 33
immaculate, p. 15
impartial, p. 9
improper, p. 72
improvident, p. 72
incense, p. 24
incense, p. 24
incinerate, p. 69
incite, p. 21
inject, p. 51
insight, p. 21
insinuate, p. 69
intimate, p. 24
intimate, p. 24
inversion, p. 45
irreversible, p. 75

jabberwocky, p. 36

kindness, p. 15
know-how, p. 18

labyrinth, p. 9
laconic, p. 27
Laundromat, p. 42
lenient, p. 12
life span p. 18
lilliputian, p. 36
loiter, p. 33
lorry, p. 60
low-key, p. 18

mackintosh, p. 60
magnolia, p. 63
majestic, p. 39
malapropism, p. 36
malice, p. 15
mandatory, p. 15
maverick, p. 27
mayonnaise, p. 30
megaphone, p. 57
mercurial, p. 63
mesmerize, p. 27
meteorologist, p. 45
microcosm, p. 72
microscope, p. 72
monsoon, p. 45
monumental, p. 39
motorcade, p. 42

narcissus, p. 36
noxious, p. 9
nucleus, p. 63

opaque, p. 12
open-ended, p. 18
orangutan, p. 33
overture, p. 48

pacify, p. 6
panacea, p. 54
pandemonium,
    p. 54
panorama, p. 54
paramount, p. 9
pawn, p. 24
pawn, p. 24
percussion, p. 48
petition, p. 9
petrol, p. 60
phonics, p. 57
plaintiff, p. 69
plaintive, p. 69
poinsettia, p. 63
poodle, p. 33
posterity, p. 15
precipitation, p. 45
prissy, p. 42
puckish, p. 36

quixotic, p. 36

radiance, p. 39
rebellion, p. 54
reject, p. 51
remorseless, p. 75
repel, p. 12
reverence, p. 15
robot, p. 36

safari, p. 33
sari, p. 21
sarong, p. 33
saturnine, p. 27
scow, p. 33
scrooge, p. 36
sensational, p. 75
sequoia, p. 27
severe, p. 12
sitcom, p. 42
skedaddle, p. 66
slovenly, p. 15
snaggletooth, p. 66
snorkel, p. 33
solar energy, p. 18
sorry, p. 21
spaniel, p. 30
staccato, p. 48
stoical, p. 75
stratus, p. 45
summit, p. 39
suppress, p. 6

surge, p. 9
surmise, p. 6
symphony, p. 57
synchronize, p. 57

tantalize, p. 63
tempo, p. 48
thingamabob, p. 66
tolerance, p. 75
topsy-turvy, p. 66
torch, p. 60
tortuous, p. 69
torturous, p. 69
transparent, p. 12
travelogue, p. 42
troubleshoot, p. 18
tulle, p. 63
turquoise, p. 30
typhoon, p. 45

unnecessary, p. 15
utopian, p. 36

valiant, p. 9
velocity, p. 75
verify, p. 6

waiver, p. 21
walkathon, p. 42
waver, p. 21
wishy-washy, p. 66
wound, p. 24
wound, p. 24

zinnia, p. 27

78

Answers

Lesson 1, page 6: A. 1. sociable, companionable 2. calm, appease 3. join, merge 4. morose, gloomy 5. proud, arrogant 6. uproar, unrest 7. quell, crush 8. confirm, authenticate **B.** 1. destiny 2. surmise

page 7: A. 1. suppress 2. verify 3. commotion 4. destiny 5. gregarious 6. glum 7. surmise 8. pacify 9. consolidate 10. haughty **B.** 1. commotion 2. prisoner 3. gregarious 4. verify **page 8:** 1. dismal, sullen, unhappy 2. tumult, agitation, disturbance 3. subdue, stop, restrain 4. infer, suppose, conjecture 5. quiet, placate, soothe

Lesson 2, page 9: A. 1. abundant 2. haggard 3. valiant 4. impartial 5. surge 6. petition 7. paramount 8. noxious **B.** 1. disciple 2. labyrinth

page 10: A. 1. noxious 2. abundant 3. surge 4. petition 5. haggard 6. impartial 7. paramount 8. valiant 9. labyrinth 10. disciple **B.** 1. complicated 2. water 3. sleeplessness 4. crusader **page 11:** 1. impartial 2. haggard 3. noxious 4. abundant 5. surge 6. valiant 7. paramount 8. labyrinth 9. petition 10. disciple

Lesson 3, page 12: A. 1. stern 2. impenetrable 3. tolerant 4. tempt 5. compatible 6. real 7. reject 8. hostile **B.** 1. opaque, obvious 2. untrue, factual **page 13: A.** 1. severe 2. fanciful 3. entice 4. lenient 5. transparent 6. factual 7. opaque 8. congenial 9. repel 10. disagreeable **B.** 1. severe 2. argument 3. gryphon 4. gauze **page 14:** lenient, congenial, fanciful, transparent, entice

Lesson 4, page 15: A. 1. needed 2. neat 3. descendants 4. respect 5. forefathers **B.** 1. discourtesy, veneration 2. meanness, consideration 3. unkempt, unsoiled 4. love, spite 5. unneeded, obligatory **page 16: A.** 1. kindness 2. mandatory 3. slovenly 4. unnecessary 5. ancestors 6. disrespect 7. immaculate 8. posterity 9. reverence 10. malice **B.** 1. posterity 2. enemy 3. teasing 4. disrespect **page 17:** 1. unnecessary 2. ancestor 3. kindness 4. malice 5. mandatory 6. immaculate 7. disrespect

8. reverence 9. slovenly 10. posterity. Riddle: minute mice

Lesson 5, page 18: A. 1. d 2. a 3. e 4. f 5. g 6. c 7. h 8. b **B.** 1. solar energy 2. health club **page 19: A.** 1. life span 2. high-rise 3. troubleshoot 4. open-ended 5. solar energy 6. health club 7. know-how 8. getaway 9. low-key 10. drive-in **B.** 1. health club 2. car 3. expert 4. drive-in **page 20:** 1. health club 2. life span 3. getaway 4. low-key 5. solar energy 6. troubleshoot 7. high-rise 8. drive-in 9. open-ended 10. know-how

Lesson 6, page 21: A. 1. hue 2. waver 3. hostile 4. sorry 5. hew 6. incite 7. insight **B.** 1. hostel 2. sari 3. waiver **page 22: A.** 1. hue 2. hostel 3. incite 4. sari 5. waver 6. hew 7. insight 8. sorry 9. waiver 10. hostile **B.** 1. waver 2. offender 3. blue 4. hostile **page 23:** 1. Mystery at the Hostile Hostel 2. If You Sign a Waiver, You Might Be Sorry 3. Insight into Hues for Your Home 4. Looking Good in a Sari 5. Don't Waver! How to Hew Out Your Share of Happiness 6. When To Incite a Rebellion

Lesson 7, page 24: A. 1. a 2. a 3. a 4. b 5. b 6. b **B.** 1. pawn 2. wound 3. wound 4. pawn **page 25: A.** 1. wound 2. incense 3. pawn 4. buffet 5. intimate 6. wound 7. buffet 8. incense 9. intimate 10. pawn **B.** 1. no 2. yes 3. yes 4. yes **page 26:** A. 2 B. 2 C. 1 D. 3 E. 2 F. 3 G. 1 H. 3 I. 1 J. 2

Lesson 8, page 27: A. 1. saturnine 2. sequoia 3. laconic 4. mesmerize 5. cardigan 6. maverick **B.** 1. d 2. c 3. a 4. b **page 28: A.** 1. boycott 2. cardigan 3. saturnine 4. derricks 5. bacitracin 6. zinnias 7. mesmerized 8. sequoia 9. maverick 10. laconic **B.** 1. protesters 2. cardigan 3. zinnia 4. dissent **page 29:** 1. sequoia 2. cardigan 3. boycott 4. laconic 5. bacitracin 6. mesmerize 7. zinnia 8. saturnine 9. maverick 10. derrick

Lesson 9, page 30: A. 1. canary 2. currants 3. turquoise 4. afghan 5. denim 6. atoll **B.** 1. c 2. d 3. b 4. a **page 31: A.** 1. cashmere 2. turquoise 3. canary 4. atoll 5. spaniel 6. currants 7. denim 8. mayonnaise

9. badminton 10. afghan **B.** 1. atoll 2. denim 3. canary 4. sandwich **page 32:** 1. spaniel 2. atoll 3. afghan 4. canary 5. mayonnaise 6. currants 7. badminton 8. cashmere 9. denim 10. turquoise

Lesson 10, page 33: A. 1. Malay 2. German 3. Malay 4. German 5. Dutch 6. Arabic **B.** 1. frolic 2. loiter 3. scow 4. safari **page 34: A.** 1. safari 2. poodle 3. loiter 4. iceberg 5. algebra 6. sarong 7. frolic 8. scow 9. snorkel 10. orangutan **B.** 1. sarong 2. iceberg 3. snorkel 4. poodle **pages 35:** 1. poodle 2. algebra 3. scow 4. loiter 5. iceberg 6. safari 7. sarong 8. frolic 9. snorkel 10. orangutan

Lesson 11, page 36: A. 1. lilliputian 2. quixotic 3. malapropism 4. robot 5. Herculean 6. scrooge **B.** 1. b 2. c 3. d 4. a **page 37: A.** 1. scrooge 2. quixotic 3. narcissus 4. robot 5. jabberwocky 6. puckish 7. Herculean 8. malapropism 9. lilliputian 10. utopian **B.** 1. malapropism 2. work 3. lilliputian 4. puckish **page 38:** 1. quixotic 2. puckish 3. narcissus 4. jabberwocky 5. Herculean 6. utopian 7. malapropism 8. robot 9. scrooge 10. scrooge

Lesson 12, page 39: A. 1. thrifty, sparing 2. criticize, scold 3. decrease, diminish 4. unconcealed, uncovered 5. huge, mammoth 6. peak, top 7. noble, imposing 8. squall, blast **B.** 1. hint 2. radiance **page 40: A.** 1. barefaced 2. radiance 3. summit 4. castigate 5. frugal 6. majestic 7. gust 8. hint 9. monumental 10. dwindle **B.** 1. saver 2. sun 3. mountain 4. majestic **page 41:** 1. frugal 2. hint 3. dwindle 4. barefaced 5. majestic 6. castigate 7. radiance 8. summit 9. gust 10. monumental. Riddle: the letter g

Lesson 13, page 42: A. 1. sitcom 2. fortnight 3. walkathon 4. prissy 5. motorcade 6. travelogue 7. flextime 8. farewell **B.** 1. clash 2. Laundromat **pages 43: A.** 1. clash 2. sitcom 3. walkathon 4. flextime 5. farewell 6. Laundromat 7. travelogue 8. motorcade 9. fortnight 10. prissy **B.** 1. walkathon 2. fortnight 3. comedy 4. dryer **page 44:** 1. Laundromat 2. farewell 3. sitcom

4. prissy 5. motorcade 6. clash 7. fortnight 8. travelogue 9. walk-athon 10. flextime

Lesson 14, page 45: A. 1. tempest 2. wet wind 3.damp air 4. reversal of air temperature 5. gusty 6. shower **B.** 1. stratus 2. meteorologist 3. cirrus 4. cumulus **page 46: A.** 1. meteorologist 2. stratus 3. humid 4. cirrus 5. typhoon 6. blustery 7. monsoon 8. inversion 9. precipitation 10. cumulus **B.** 1. umbrella 2. cumulus 3. predict 4. wet **page 47:** Clouds: 1. stratus 2. cirrus 3. cumulus Winds: 4. blustery 5. typhoon 6. monsoon People: 7. meteorologist Other: 8. humid 9. inversion 10. precipitation

Lesson 15, page 48: A. 1. rapid 2. drum 3. interrupted 4. introduction 5. moderate 6. melody **B.** 1. d 2. c 3. b 4. a **pages 49: A.** 1. overture 2. crescendo 3. tempo 4. aria 5. allegro 6. percussion 7. clef 8. adagio 9. staccato 10. chords **B.** 1. aria 2. beginning 3. cymbals 4. increase **page 50:** Across: 3. percussion 6. staccato 9. allegro 10. overture Down: 1. clef 2. aria 4. crescendo 5. adagio 7. chord 8. tempo

Lesson 16, page 51: A. 1. delight, fulfill 2. surmise, suppose 3. introduce, insert 4. repudiate, discard 5. appreciation, gratefulness 6. presentation, hearing 7. compliment, praise **B.** 1. auditorium 2. audience 3. audible **page 52: A.** 1. audition 2. reject 3. audible 4. conjecture 5. audience 6. inject 7. gratitude 8. gratify 9. auditorium 10. congratulate **B.** 1. audition 2. gratitude 3. rotten 4. graduate **page 53:** 1. gratify 2. reject 3. audible 4. inject 5. audience 6. auditorium 7. audition 8. congratulate 9. conjecture 10. gratitude

Lesson 17, page 54: A. 1. rebellion 2. panacea 3. belligerent 4. pandemonium 5. panorama 6. aerate 7. aeronautics 8. aerial **B.** 1. <u>aero</u>dynamics 2. <u>aero</u>bics **page 55: A.** 1. panorama 2. belligerent 3. aerobics 4. pandemonium 5. aerial 6. panacea 7. aerodynamics 8. rebellion 9. aerate 10. aeronautics **B.** 1. roof 2. gym 3. anger 4. confusion **page 56:**

1. panacea 2. rebellion 3. belligerent 4. panorama 5. aerial 6. aerodynamics 7. pandemonium 8. aerobics 9. aeronautics 10. aerate

Lesson 18, page 57: A. 1. b 2. c 3. f 4. g 5. d 6. e 7. a **B.** 1. <u>phon</u>ics 2. <u>chron</u>ology 3. ana<u>chron</u>ism

page 58: A. 1. chronology 2. euphonious 3. symphony 4. anachronism 5. megaphone 6. synchronize 7. chronic 8. cacophony 9. phonics 10. chronicle **B.** 1. anachronism 2. megaphone 3. birdsong 4. orchestra **page 59:** 1. correspond, match, coincide 2. babel, discordant, jarring 3. ongoing, persistent, unremitting 4. melodious, tuneful, harmonious 5. record, account, narrative

Lesson 19, page 60: A. 1. diversion 2. petrol 3. torch 4. dustbin 5. braces 6. mackintosh **B.** 1. lorry 2. chips 3. crumpet 4. cinema

page 61: A. 1. chips 2. braces 3. mackintosh 4. lorry 5. cinema 6. petrol 7. torch 8. diversion 9. crumpet 10. dustbin **B.** 1. diversion 2. petrol 3. lorry 4. pants

page 62: 1 .mackintosh, raincoat 2. cinema, movie 3. braces, suspenders 4. petrol, gas 5. torch, flashlight 6. diversion, detour 7. dustbin, trash can 8. crumpet, muffin 9. chips, French fries 10. lorry, truck

Lesson 20, page 63: A. 1. blazer 2. boulevard 3. coward 4. nucleus 5. tulle 6. flamingo

B. 1. d 2. a 3. b 4. c **page 64: A.** 1. boulevards 2. flamingo 3. coward 4. tantalize 5. tulle 6. magnolia 7. mercurial 8. blazers 9. nucleus 10. poinsettia **B.** 1. flamingo 2. traffic 3. blazer 4. hide **page 65:** 1. blazer 2. tulle 3. tantalize 4. mercurial 5. magnolia 6. flamingo 7. boulevard 8. poinsettia 9. coward 10. coward

Lesson 21, page 66: A. 1. flutter 2. guffaw 3. clean 4. hairless 5. doubt 6. calm 7. ungrammatical **B.** 1. snaggletooth 2. hunky-dory 3. hootenanny **page 67: A.** 1. gewgaw 2. snaggletooth 3. wishy-washy 4. topsy-turvy 5. hootenanny 6. hunky-dory 7. balderdash 8. thingamabob 9. skedaddle 10. flummox **B.** 1. pin 2. hootenanny 3. coward 4. skedaddle **page 68:**

1. flummox 2. hunky-dory 3. hootenanny 4. snaggletooth 5. wishy-washy 6. gewgaw 7. thingamabob 8. topsy-turvy 9. skedaddle 10. balderdash

Lesson 22, page 69: A. 1. insinuate 2. alley 3. tortuous 4. desolate 5. dissolute 6. torturous 7. ally 8. plaintive **B.** 1. incinerate 2. plaintiff **page 70: A.** 1. desolate 2. tortuous 3. incinerates 4. ally 5. plaintive 6. insinuate 7. alley 8. torturous 9. dissolute 10. plaintiff **B.** 1. ally 2. airstrip 3. desolate 4. song

page 71: Across: 1. plaintive 5. alley 6. incinerate 7. tortuous 8. dissolute 9. desolate Down: 1. plaintiff 2. ally 3. insinuate 4. torturous

Lesson 23, page 72: A. 1. wisdom 2. imprudent 3. unfriendly 4. unseemly 5. lower 6. presage **B.** 1. de 2. micro 3. micro 4. anti **page 73: A.** 1. improper 2. desegregate 3. foreshadow 4.antisocial 5. improvident 6. foresight 7. microcosm 8.devalue 9. antitoxin 10. microscope **B.** 1.improper 2. planning 3. foreshadow 4. spendthrift **page 74:** 1. a missile that intercepts and destroys other missiles 2. relieve of pressure 3. predict 4. a strong feeling of aversion 5. film on which photographed material is greatly reduced in size 6. predecessor 7. not movable 8. not measurable 9. thaw 10. instrument that amplifies sound by converting acoustical waves into electric current

Lesson 24, page 75: A. 1. stoical 2. remorseless 3. arrogance 4. velocity 5. sensational 6. defenseless 7. tolerance 8. irreversible **B.** 1. convert<u>ible</u> 2. hospita<u>lity</u> **page 76: A.** 1. remorseless 2. velocity 3. tolerance 4. hospitality 5. defenseless 6. irreversible 7. sensational 8. stoical 9. convertible 10. arrogance **B.** 1. inn 2. sensational 3. convertible 4. infant **page 77:** Answers will vary.